WOMEN:
THE FINAL FRONTIER

GW00802067

WOMEN: THE FINAL FRONTIER

Everything a Man Needs to Know

Robert Withe, Alan Fredricks
and Denzil Lewis

RIGHT WAY

Typeset in 11/12½pt Times by Letterpart Limited, Reigate, Surrey.

Printed and bound in Great Britain by Cox & Wyman Ltd., Reading, Berkshire.

The *Right Way* series is published by Elliot Right Way Books, Brighton Road, Lower Kingswood, Tadworth, Surrey, KT20 6TD, U.K. For information about our company and the other books we publish, visit our web site at www.right-way.co.uk

CONTENTS

INTRODUCTION

It began, like all good ideas, in a late-night kebab house in central London. The three of us were happily re-fuelling after a stimulating evening of forming relationships with attractive women.

Looking around us, we could not help noticing the miserable faces of fellow night-owls, and remembered when we wore the same looks of frustration and failure as a matter of habit.

It wasn't easy for us to gain confidence with women. We all started with blank slates, fresh-faced innocents in the art of fulfilling the desires of the opposite sex. We are three ordinary guys with no more power than it takes to flag a taxi, who have never been in the upper tax bracket and who lead such low-key lives even our local papers have never mentioned us. Worse, we all began with basic hang-ups and delusions about the dating game that held us back. We endured years of loneliness, attending countless social functions with no female company in tow, being constantly ribbed by enemies and friends about our single status, sitting at the front rows of cinemas with only popcorn boxes for company.

Motivated by misery, we set out on the road of change. The journey was long, twisting and not made easier by countless mistimed pit-stops. Clubs, bars, parties, activity groups, introductory agencies – we did all the scenarios and, early on, did them badly. To our credit, we never gave up. More to the point, we learned well from our mistakes. Eventually, after meeting hundreds of women of different ages, races and cultures, the way ahead became smooth, straight and the road-signs to intimacy were easy to read. Now, after a combined thirty years of hard-earned experience we feel qualified to answer the crucial male questions: *What do women want?* and *How do you give it to them?*

These were dilemmas that clearly worried the men around us. Men who probably deserved some solid information to get them beyond the hit and miss approach to relationship forming. No such source had been on offer when we started out. Instead, we red-bloods had to make do with pheromone sprays, chat-up books and other dubious quick fixes which preyed on anxieties and ignored pressing modern-day issues such as salary differences, changing gender roles, contraception, sexually transmitted diseases and behavioural science. Most annoyingly, the most relevant issue, the only one that all the different branches of feminism agree on, was hardly mentioned: women, like nightclub managements, *always* reserve the right to choose.

.As we sat chomping away, we concluded that it was surely time for some form of accessible and mature consultation on this important area of life, because no man should have to suffer like we did to learn what we now know. And here is the reality of our collective idea. It is an intimacy manual, dedicated to forming fulfilling relationships with female strangers. It will enable you to make a fresh start, away from the mixed messages of work colleagues, or guilty feelings about wanting your best friend's partner and, equally, save you begging your sister to set you up with her friends.

This is the book we would love to have read back when dating was so tough for us – when we each began with our first girlfriends. As a result, we accept that we may deal with some topics in a manner more serious than some readers might expect. Of course, we are the first to agree that all dating *should* be fun; however, it has to be said that only those men who make the fewest mistakes can afford to appear wholly laid back in the art of meeting and greeting, and this is why we have flagged some advice within these pages

"CAUTION: HANDLE WITH CARE". We want you to be aware that there may be tricky ground so that you can limit any likelihood of emotional hurt to yourself or others.

Included here are hundreds of workable lines that can be used to further conversation, practical methods of boosting your confidence with women, realistically-scripted scenarios to suit many situations, kitten-heel perspectives to show life through women's eyes, effective ways to find compatible partners, and bull's-eye reasoning to back-up our advocacy. Make no mistake, this is not a book of pap psychology; it won't put hairs on your chest, make you grow bigger biceps or add an extra inch where you think it's most needed; but every single one of the principles set out has been road-tested to success.

You won't need the determination of an Arctic explorer to put them into effect either; the only trait required is something you have already shown – a willingness to change. Change to what, you may ask? Well, you're not expected to transform into an attention-grabbing superlad or to focus on any one type of outlook. Trendy cynicism, for example, can make you give up; old-fashioned romanticism can make her throw up. If, however, you can combine the two, to become a realistic romantic, you will make the most of your opportunities. And as far as we're concerned, this approach does *not* include hurting women to make them comply with your intimate needs. It is true that relationships have so much potential for pleasure that, inevitably, they can also cause pain; but with effective use of the information presented here, it is our earnest hope that neither you nor your future partners will find cause for unacceptable grief.

In the final analysis, we remain three ordinary men. Yet, by finding ways to attract women that bring out the best of ourselves and provide the right balance between what women want and what we can give them, we have formed many mutually-satisfying relationships.

If we can do it . . .

1

THE WAY THINGS ARE

What do women want above all? Men. All women, from tots playing with well-formed dolls, through teenagers experimenting with lip gloss, to power dressing thirty-somethings, are bombarded with information on how to make themselves more attractive to men. And this information is put to good use as modern women hit the social scene, mix through chosen sports or recreations, go on holidays, or join agencies and place personal ads with the sole aim of meeting the hairier sex.

Men remain the main topic of discussion when single women get together and (at least until cloning clinics open for business) the male contribution to conception is as necessary as wheels on a car. Add to this any number of contemporary bestseller books which would be reduced to leaflets if the main plot line of getting Mr Right was removed. We could go on, but the point is made. In these days of changing gender roles, the rise and rise of the single woman and the increase of male insecurities, it is important not to overlook the simple truth that *women want men*.

Granted, the details – how long women want men for, how many they want, if they will continue to want men in the future and what makes them want Joe and not Fred – are a wee bit trickier.

They are not quite as complex, though, as consistent rejection and sloppy advice can make men think, and we will prove this in due course. Mainly, you should ground yourself in the unshakeable truth about overall female desire for men. Do this and you will always have a solid base to work from.

Another fundamental truth, less obvious in these days of niche markets and specialised websites, is that women's relationship needs are universal, varying in scale, not context. Take commitment, possibly the most well-known need. To some women it means marriage, to others it means a second opinion while shopping, but every woman wants a partner who places her first and won't be unfaithful.

Once you are comfortable with what women's needs really are, women will be comfortable with you.

DESIRE

Okay, so women want men. Why, then, are they so fussy? Or to look at it from her angle, why are men so damn slack? Why do women in short skirts cause more reaction than men in shorts, even though men's legs are on view less often on the high street? Why did a survey of over 18,000 adults indicate that 1% of men form relationships with 16% of the available women? And yet, why do British Juliets regularly receive millions more Valentine's cards than would-be Romeos? Because, in our opinion, desire flows from a *combination* of the only real influences on all human behaviour: biology and conditioning.

Biology

The men in white coats have such a dry approach to relationships one can't help wondering how they conduct their own. Scientific literature is not exactly flush with the joys of arranging dates, the simple pleasure of taking turns to cook dinner, or the glow of achievement that comes from reaching an anniversary. But the scientists do put forward a lot of arguments and speculation about relationships that make sense, especially when it comes to gender difference.

Their starting point is our genes, the bio-chemical units of heredity. Everything that lives or has ever lived is composed of genes. Genes themselves are not "alive" in the conscious way that higher animals (yes, that includes you) are, but considering they existed billions of years before men even walked upright, it is reasonable to assume genes must have some fail-safe method of ensuring their survival. That method, for birds, bees and educated fleas, is sex, or to be exact, procreation. Beyond the emotional fireworks, physical hydraulics and springing beds, sex ensures that any offspring will have a new, unique genetic mixture.

It was once thought that the purpose of this mixing (and therefore of sex) was to fuel the engine of ecological evolution, allowing man to adapt to his environment and to protect himself against other beasts. But the most potent danger to man has always been from microscopic predators, the viruses and bacteria that are the chief causes of disease. The ''Spanish flu'' epidemic of 1918, for example, killed almost twice as many people as died in the First World War. And so opinion has been shifting towards a school of thought that sex actually exists to combat internal hazards, not surrounding ones.

Most bacteria are in fact beneficial, but both harmless and harmful microbes go forth and multiply at a fantastic rate. For example, in one day, an E-coli bacterium has the potential via a sexless process known as binary fission – where a bacterium grows until it splits into two genetically-identical copies – to turn into well over six million others.

If all bacteria were clones, the reproduction rate would not be so worrying. Find a drug that kills a bacterium and, theoretically, you can wipe out the whole species. Indeed, humans have many inborn defences against specific diseases. However, one way in which bacteria evolve (i.e. possibly change into more virulent infections) is by mutating. This is where playing the numbers game by fission instead of sex is to their advantage. The random mutation rates of bacteria range from one in a million to one in a billion. Given that there are billions of bacteria in any adult's body, they can evolve as much in one person's lifetime as people have in the last million years!

If humans and larger animals are to keep pace with this constant threat, the collective genetic urge for sex must be strong. And it is. It has been estimated that two-thirds of the human brain is hard-wired to respond to sexual stimuli.

However, despite all your genes having a stake in procreation it doesn't pay to make the sexual urge all-consuming. There are other priorities, such as finding food, building shelters and filing tax returns, that are necessary for the survival of the host. Fortunately, because partner sex is an urge, as distinct from a necessity like breathing, man has *some* degree of control over it. Abstaining monks and uninterested nuns, for example, have decided not to indulge at all.

If both monks and nuns gave in to the carnal urge, it is almost certain their ways of choosing partners would be different. According to science, this split is due to the oldest gender difference of all: women bear children, men don't.

Science speculates that women are genetically "programmed" to be choosier with whom they have sex because they have a bigger investment in the outcome. Even on a conscious level, a woman knows that pregnancy is nine months out of her reproductive lifetime. It seems that this is why women are less easily aroused, so that they can retain their senses during courtship and make more accurate partner choices. We will expand on the meaning of "accurate" later. Meanwhile, men are thought to have a greater urge for partners because that raises the chances of having their own children. This strategy would have been formed in prehistory – i.e. thousands of years before blood-testing – when only a woman could be sure a child was hers.

No-one can say how wide the gaps of these "desire differences" are between men and women, boys and girls. You may have seen first hand that women's minds can occasionally be consumed with lust, but it is more likely your experiences amount to an appreciation of men being the sexually impulsive gender. On the whole, it seems that women are naturally the more selective sex. Despite all the social changes that have given women more sexual freedom, we agree with the scientists that these essential differences in desire won't change. At least, not until the genes do.

Conditioning

Rather than attacking culture as a man-made artefact, the new breed of behavioural researchers are suggesting that conformity is as genetic as skin colour. If the urge to be like others is natural, it explains why location and vocation have a lot of influence on the way women behave. What non-biological argument can otherwise explain why a UK marriage is seven times more likely to end in divorce than an Italian one, why nurses have a greater sexual reputation than librarians or why women from Newcastle (you'll have to trust us here) are easier to approach than women from London? Or why, in all the above groups, the women will each have at least one embarrassing girlhood photo, showing what passed for sartorial elegance once but, with the benefit of (conformed) hindsight, looks like a fashion mistake now? These points all add weight to the idea of a genetic basis for following social convention.

Social rules and laws have traditionally been made by men, for men, and have restricted women far more. For example, the first English divorce occurred in 1670 but it was not until 1923 that women were granted full rights to divorce on the same grounds as men. Equality legislation, the pill and economic opportunities have brought women's lifestyles closer to men's, but they still lag behind men in being able to do what they want (go for a late night walk); go where they want (how many women do you see on their own in pubs?); say what they want (forget about the views of famous women who are free to air their views and then duck behind the barricade of cele*"bra"*ty – real women are still careful about divulging their sexual desires in mixed company); and get what they feel they deserve (women still mostly get paid a quarter less than men for doing the same job).

Despite the social changes and media gossip that they are the new sexual predators, women in Britain still have to take factors like reputation into account. As long as the terms "slapper" and "stud" keep their distance as insult and compliment, women will always be more worried about what others think. No, it doesn't stop women playing the field, but it does make them play quietly.

Spread your net

Women have little time for genetic explanations of the infamous male aversion to commitment. No surprise there because, not only does she want to be the only one but also, as we have been lucky enough to find out, one partner is capable of satisfying all a man's intimate needs. Prior to any real commitment though, you cannot afford to attach too much importance to any one woman. Like it or not, she may not (yet) attach the same importance to you. Unfounded high hopes can cause crushing defeats. To counter this outcome, spread your *pre-intimate* relationship desires as widely as possible. You will stand more chance of relaxing on your date with Jane if you know that you are going to see Samantha the next day.

Effective net-spreading is about calming yourself, not showing off. There's no need for ill-mannered flaunting of your popularity with other girlfriends, unless perhaps Jane seems to think you are incapable of attracting anyone else!

It should go without saying, however, that once you make a shared commitment, your joint interests are best served by ceasing to chase other women. Okay, it's easier said than done – but then the right thing is always the hardest to do.

No

You now know the arguments for female choosiness – so always be aware that no woman has to desire you simply because you desire her. The word "no" must always be taken seriously. It might be the one word men hate hearing most but you **must** listen, however much you feel she is just playing hard to get. We don't dispute that women often display relationship guile, and that they generally feel that some resistance must be shown to keep dignity. But there is no room here for ambiguity; when she says "no", back off.

Nothing is stopping you from trying to reassure her that your desire for intimacy means no emotional or physical harm. If you do this, she *may* let you try again but, in these sexually harassing times, you cannot afford to subscribe to the "no means yes'' theory. Thinking like a bully will only get you a custodial sentence, and you'd deserve it.

Giving

A staple ingredient of romantic fiction is that men walk away from women far more than in real life. You may be painfully aware of the spiralling divorce rates and that seven out of ten divorce actions are initiated by women. Less well-known is the fact that most women divorce on the grounds of unreasonable behaviour. Undoubtedly, on average, men are less sensitive and caring than women (most nurses are women, most teachers too, and all mothers) and greater economic opportunities have made it easier for women to leave destructive relationships but – and we almost hesitate to say this – the blame cannot lie solely with men. The late nineties culture of ''Gimme, gimme, gimme'' has not been the ideal atmosphere for long-term relationships, and it has exaggerated the basic truth. Namely that the desire differences allow women to demand more from men, because men are more willing to supply. It may seem that this is a new event but in our view it has just been masked by the old con tricks of keeping women down, making them feel insecure and making them feel glad that any man is interested in them.

Over and above desire, the reality needs to be conceded that the structure of marital relationships has swung firmly towards women's control. It is interesting [now] to note that before the divorce laws were changed in 1923, six out of ten divorces were instigated by men.

To combat the current lack of compromise from both sides, some therapists have voiced the premise that men and women should learn to accept their differences rather than trying to change each sex into a clone of the other. Such thoughts are noble, but, in our experience, unworkable. The only way women will stop expecting unequal attention is if men down tools and stop giving it! This is as likely as men queuing up for voluntary castration, and one-man protests by you won't make any impact either. However proud or aloof you are in the company of other lads, an inflexible attitude won't help you make contact with the girl you want. Any man who wants to relate well to women has to be prepared to give. In the short term, this means being the one prepared to make the first move, the first to express feelings and the first to commit. In the long run, it means being prepared to give as much commitment as it takes.

Expectation

Men often tout this air of expectation among women – at least in the short term – as one of the most unfair aspects of the dating game. Please don't fall into this trap of self-pity. Women would love to be free to approach any man they desire. Imagine if, as one day may be the case, it was accepted and expected for women to approach men? How many men would be left on the shelf, like the plain woman with attractive friends? Even with those women bold enough to make approaches now, there is no guarantee that you'll desire them. The prevailing conditions of female expectation and male action are still in your favour and you should be prepared to make use of this.

Games

A widely held perception is that women view a relationship as a game of clay-court tennis, while, for men, it's more like a work-out in the gym. A diplomatic reason given is that flirtation, for example, is used by women as a kind of vetting process, to test how suitable a man is. This is not even half the story. Women also play games with men because they enjoy it. Not because they are witches and bitches, but because it is one area of life where they have always had a chance of winning. The desire difference makes men vulnerable to being taken advantage of. Advantage-taking is human nature, from world-wide territorial conflict to holding on to a neighbour's power drill. It takes a very disciplined woman not to play games, and modern women are not encouraged to hold back. What really counts is how much the games are designed to hurt.

At least flirtation is flattering, as it is usually motivated by some sort of affection. Teasing is a different matter and is, we fear, done mainly to boost the ego at some poor unfortunate's expense. However adept you become at relating to women, you will always be susceptible to being taken for a ride. Still, you should only be teased by the same woman once. How often do you need to step on a garden rake before you avoid doing it? A tease will often return to the scene of the crime, but once you show resistance to her wiles, she, and all other female observers of this game, will increase their respect for you.

HER PERSONALITY
In the long run, personality is more important than sex and, with such a heavy current premium on time, searching for suitable partners has to be as much about perception as determination. You may never truly know what a woman is like until you're in a relationship but there are ways to assess if she's someone you want to choose furniture with. Strangely enough, feminism helps your cause here. Female empowerment is not quite the penis guillotine some would have you believe. In fact, it has blown women's cover because it actively encourages women to be themselves. This makes it easier for men to decide which women are worth chasing and which are not.

When you meet women, personality clues are usually there in front of you. Pay attention . . .

Equal weight
The logical method of accurate male choice is to give beauty and personality equal weight. Pity there is often such a divide between rationale and instinct! While "lay" men may explain their preference for physical appeal purely on the basis of eye-candy stimulation, biologists, as we might expect, strip everything down to the essentials of reproduction. They claim instead that somewhere, deep within the male psyche, is the inherent understanding that youth and beauty equal vitality. They go on to suggest that certain types of hip-to-waist ratios, perky breasts and flat stomachs are widely attractive because they are shapely signposts of fertility. Take that as you will,

women, of course, don't need any telling about the importance of beauty. Nearly ninety pence of every pound spent on cosmetic surgery goes on improving the female form.

It seems to be so ingrained in men to "see with glee", that the principle of awarding equal weight to personality may take you time to develop. To start with, don't tell any beautiful girl how impressive she looks until you have struck a rapport. Let the warmth of her personality earn any compliments you give. Other methods of balancing looks and character are given later.

Without doubt, giving equal weight is the most difficult principle you will read in this book. That's why the rewards are enormous if you can put it into practice. Once women realise that you are far more interested in the total package, those who use sex as power will tend to steer well clear, while well-adjusted women will be drawn to you.

Compatibility

Everybody knows life is smoother the more you have in common with others, so why do some women go for men who are so obviously wrong for them? Phrases like "low self-esteem", "charming manipulator", "a bit naïve" and "desperate for anyone" may have their place, but they also deny that the woman might, just might, be in full control of her actions. From where we stand, compatibility is not just about a shared sense of fashion or music taste, it's also about power. We are not writing about the top-of-the-tree power that drives self-made women, nor the specialised type of power that involves whips, fluffy handcuffs and thigh-length boots, but the emotional prestige that all people crave because it makes them feel worthwhile.

A woman will think carefully about how much power she gains by being seen in your company (will she be raised in the estimation of other women for attracting you?), about how much power you are willing to give (can you say sorry, or purposely lose an argument to make her feel good?) and about how much power you are willing to take (can you stamp your foot down if she proposes a weekend trip with her ex-boyfriend?).

The man who behaves as if he is pinned with a shiny

prefect's badge – always insisting upon being in the right – has no understanding of women's need for power.

While no woman goes into a relationship wanting to be mistreated, that doesn't mean she wants a perfect man either. Ideal men take away the pleasure of modification and magnify the insecurities of the imperfect other half. Added to this, women don't just look for parallel characteristics in partners, but complementary ones as well. That's why it can seem that opposites attract. Gentle women sometimes go for men who are assertive enough to do what they can't, like slam the phone down on a cold-calling salesman or return the dysfunctional goods to the store; while pushy women end up with push-overs.

There is, then, much more to compatibility than enjoying the same sense of humour, and the quicker you can find out if you fit her frame the better. Search for patterns in her previous relationships and watch out for the types to whom she seems attracted. Think hard about whether you might be prepared to adapt in any permanent way.

Assumptions
The accuracy of your assumptions about her is important, but so is correctly gauging her assumptions about you. For example, the problem with women that you know is that they *think* they know you. Forming relationships with these women involves fighting an uphill struggle against the incredible strength of female assumption. Women believe that they are more emotionally astute than men and, if the ability to judge character is any measure, they have a point. However, while it's true that women are intuitive, they are not telepathic. Just like men, they use assumptions to fill in the blanks and, just like men, they often get it wrong. The one thing that all women definitely get right is acquiring the certain knowledge that men need women. Hence, if you have been single for a while, women who know you may have all sorts of negative assumptions about your ability to convert desire into a relationship. It's not impossible to turn around these assumptions, but, outside of Christmas work parties, it is difficult.

Female strangers are different, having no prior experience on which to base any assessment. In itself this should make you feel more confident about meeting them. And, in one of life's great loops of self-esteem, if knowing this makes you confident enough to approach a woman, you should be aware that she will assume you're confident just because you approached.

Once you have an idea what a woman's assumptions are, be prepared to accentuate the positives and deal with the negatives.

Competitive women

If you believe the hype, "New Woman" has recently fastened the masculine trait of competitiveness onto her personality. This is media-driven rubbish. Women have always competed against other women. Only now it's open season on inter-gender competition too, with women taking on men in all areas of the social sphere. But something is still clearly wrong. Though female pilots, politicians and even pugilists have proved there is no "traditional" male skill that women can't master, women aren't yet getting the competitive benefits of work that equality was supposed to bring them. Money and its making still seem to have a male bias. Any comprehensive "Rich List", or gender pie-chart of low-income employees, will show this to be the case. The generality of this money rule continues to back perhaps the most hotly-disputed theory of evolutionary science. Namely, that in Britain work and pay differences between men and women are not just the result of some cultural glass ceiling but do in fact have a biological basis as they do elsewhere in the world.

Before any aggrieved party writes in to complain, we want to make it clear that we are not suggesting men are better suited to the world of work than women. We are also aware that pay inequalities have their roots in women's work being historically undervalued – and that research *does* suggest men and women have evolved different talents. Gender seems to have little bearing on the market value of services given. Childcare, for example, may be a job where productivity is hard to measure, but it's also a job from which mothers can't easily resign.

Our own particular career experiences bear out (at least to us!) that men and women certainly have unique abilities but we think that gene-programming is not the only factor. As suggested earlier, conditioning plays a huge part. Not only are men socially trained from early ages to compete against each other rather than women (mixed school football teams are still a rarity). They also have to build up a life-skill – one to which women are oblivious – and that is at the same time at the core of this book: *learning to deal with the constant threat of initial (or subsequent) rejection by women.*

Women may actually be more scared of rejection than men but the plain fact is that an approach by Jane is likely to be better received than one made by Joe. This is not a plea for pity. It's simply an opinion that reminds us how factors such as conditioning lead to very real differences in the overall make-up of men and women. These differences are impossible to ignore once you accept the premise of science that our genes rely on procreation for survival. Following this premise places in perspective the notion that men should be more competitive than women. The desire differences explained earlier mean that men have to do more to attract partners (at least for the foreseeable future) and this same premise provides us the background clue as to why greater inborn drive can be as much an asset to men as bigger tails are to peacocks.

As long as this aspect of biology is reinforced by society, men and women will, in practice, always compete on different levels. Understanding this will help immunise your brain against the media obsession with "the dominant female" which does nothing to promote harmony between the sexes.

The money-pot may not be fully open to women, but they have always been well-equipped to wrestle with men in the relationship arena. For one thing, research points to women being better communicators than men and, for another, though female assertion may seem a new phenomenon, women have always been the sex most practised at saying no. The problem is that many women are recognising this and, even though they may feel hampered from leading the way in the office, they are more than ready to take on (or take it out on) men in the bar. This shouldn't be a worry if you're willing to roll with them rather than try to roll them over. Check out these disarming initial encounters:

You: Hi! Just thought I'd say –
Her: Oh, here we go – it's chat up time!
You: Sounds like you've been looking forward to it!
Her: Not really, not coming from you anyway.
You: Ah well; I'm here now, and my lines are all prepared so it's a shame to waste them . . .

You: Hello I –
Her: (smile) Goodbye.
You: (smile) There's no need for that. I just got here.
Her: Oh! Okay: you can stay.

Even with pleasant body language which lets you know she is not *that* serious, the competitive woman's lack of traditional femininity can be off-putting. However, all they really want (really, really want) is to enjoy themselves as much as possible. This only creates problems if they *always* want to enjoy themselves at your expense. With this sub-group of competitive women who *always* want to outdo you, your best bet is just to avoid them. You have a choice too. Ladettes and their like are not the only available women, just the loudest.

Certainly, you should not allow yourself to be intimidated by overly-competitive women. Neither should you be unduly affected by the bar-room feminists who immediately take up a humourless, anti-man position in conversation, despite not being provoked. Such severe attitudes have more to do with personal problems than cultural enlightenment. Why else go into a social environment where it is traditional for men to approach women and be cranky once approached? You can draw the sting out of her animosity by pointing out her logical error in assuming all men are the same and asking whether she would like it if you insisted that all women are gold-diggers or teasers.

Likewise, even though you may not realise it, you have the potential to deal with all sorts of unnecessary "competition". If she tries to drink you under the table, then let her; medically, your constitution is designed to handle the poisons far better than is hers. If she boasts that she earns more than you, then you can suggest cheekily that she buy the drinks or contribute more towards the meal. If she brags that she's had more relationships than you, there's no need to degenerate into name-calling. Just tell her *that* argument is as pointless as saying that men are taller than women.

Generally, however, even allowing for the women who take pains to hide their attraction because they don't want to open themselves up to rejection, if a woman likes you, she won't compete *too* much. If she doesn't really like you, then she probably will.

Arrogance

Hot on the heels of over-competitiveness, arrogance can set female assumptions in concrete and this is such a pompous barrier to conversation it can easily put men off the chase. It is also quite common and you will have to deal with it if you want to attract modernettes.

Before aggressive feminism kicked in, men accused of lacking understanding could justifiably claim the defence of female reticence. How was a man to know how much women craved the first thrust of sexual penetration when it was considered indecent for women to talk about such matters? How was he expected not to take lack of trust personally when women shouted for trustworthy men in public, but refused to open up in private? How could he know it was acceptable to make mistakes around women when praise from women was so hard to come by?

Now, women are megaphone-vocal about what they want, and that old excuse sounds, and is, lame.

Unfortunately, reticence has not always been replaced by honesty. Again, media hype about gender role-change, whipped up by brain-free journalism, bombards us daily with its "Watch out, the women are coming" distortion of the real world. Inevitably, because the nature of this onslaught has been so pervasive and persistent over at least two generations, there is a proportion of easily-led women who believe this fantasy view of world order. Some of them are so busy promoting themselves as paid-up members of the Amazon planet – "I only go for good-looking men", "I've never been dumped", "Men can't handle me because I'm strong" – and other conceited guff, that they completely lose sight of the fact that there has never been a better time to be open about what they *really* want with men.

Men have taken, on the other hand, such a constant psychological battering that many have in turn lost track of where they stand, although at the same time they may accept the need for some change. Unfortunately, there is no referee in this particular ring, and the militant feminists and their followers keep on looking for the knockout punch.

On the face of it, why shouldn't women continue to be arrogant? They now perceive that smoker's breath, pear-shapes, children in tow and lower-income status aren't the barriers to attractiveness that they once were. Their [female media] role models appear to be making a good job of having it all and their equally arrogant friends seem to be in total control of their relationships (to admit otherwise would be a sign of weakness).

Neither is it just the need to keep up with her peers and heroines that reinforces the outlook of the "superior" woman. Despite all the publicity about emasculation, many women think the male ego is as bullish as ever. Why else should the vertically-challenged man with the weak chin approach the towering beauty with the hour-glass figure? And why should he continue talking to her even though her body language screams zero interest?

Where does he get the ego?!

Some women, incidentally, do understand about the current male crisis of confidence, but still don't give a flying proverbial. *As far as they're concerned*, what do men really have to worry about? Men can walk the streets free of sexual assault, can have children until they are 210, still out-earn women, can enjoy a quiet drink without fear of seduction and may have sex with whom they want, when they want, as often as they want, without fear of recriminations.

Blinkered, one-sided mentalities like this are severely unattractive but the weird twist is that our experiences show it is more productive to persevere with an arrogant woman than a competitive one. Any woman who regularly socialises with her friends knows that men prefer women who don't treat chat-ups like border disputes.

Arrogance is less about how a girl feels towards you, more about the image she wants to portray. Shy women, for example, and there are still many, will often fake arrogance as a compensation technique. It's shy women's way of dealing with the irritating under-estimation and patronising attitudes from men that their natural reserve attracts.

How, then, do you deal with arrogance? Not with your own, that's for sure. This bears repeating – being positive is essential but the day of the arrogant male is over. If you both have a "Why-should-I?" attitude, then neither of you "will". Instead you need to see arrogance for the cultural bravado it is, rather than (however understandably) flaring up when you encounter it. Her ego, just like yours, is deceptively fragile. The hard-boiled front of arrogance has simply replaced reticence as a new way of masking this very human, and very real, vulnerability.

Her: Women don't need men; they want them.
Negative: That's rubbish – you'll always need us!
Positive: Well . . . it's great to be wanted.

Her: I've had loads of boyfriends.
Negative: You know what that makes you!
Positive: (smile) I thought you looked familiar . . .

Her: Men are useless.
Negative: Yeah – we take after our mothers!
Positive: (smile) Have we dated before?

Change

You may have realised the importance of change but the
women you meet may not. Once you've got through all the
mood and front to see her true emotional colours, don't expect
her to change them for you. Change is possible, but can't be
forced by anyone other than the person who needs to undergo
it. Her core personality has probably been set by patterns that
existed long before you came on the scene. If it doesn't suit
you, and she doesn't try to change, move on.

Trust

Gaining a woman's trust isn't easy and men tend to take lack
of it too personally. Don't. Try to appreciate that her trust may
have been shattered by ex-partners or by other significant men
in her life, such as relatives. Her experiences may have been a
touch more traumatic than mere male forgetfulness leading to
her always having to put the toilet seat down in the family
bathroom. In addition, there is the simple matter of pride.
Women are understandably reluctant to relate experiences
which may place them in a bad light. It will take time before
you can decide if any lack of trust is a problem between you.

SUPERFICIALS

Traditionally, wealth, status and looks all come below personality on the list of female desires – a state of affairs that may
be due more to diplomacy than honesty. Supermodels, for
example, are not known for forming relationships with unemployed gurners. Such tendencies are often casually dismissed
as mercenary, but that is much too simplistic. Women – the

world over – will readily pair up with pug-faced millionaires.

Only by returning to the primeval differences of childbirth and weaning can these needs be fully understood. Men may dig the tunnels, build houses and lay the pipes but the natural responsibility of childcare makes women the practical sex. Generally, from a woman's standpoint, the "superficials" can give her or her children a better quality of life; so they are not shallow at all, but sensible. As cold-blooded as these desires may seem, they would not work if they didn't trigger emotions.

In the genetic sense, emotions are simply mechanisms that make people react. The "laboratory" explanation is that women have in-built mechanisms for responding to material signs, be it to the number of kills a hunter makes or the price of an executive's car. Disregarding the importance of the superficials is one of the great con tricks that even some feminists have fallen for. It is only once you know the true worth of such desires that you can gear your ambitions and/or your other attributes to compensate for any lack.

Wealth

From slaying dragons to watching her back at the cashpoint machines, protection has always been high on every woman's agenda. And nothing protects like money. Women are under-represented at the top of the earnings scale and make up most of those on low incomes. Between these extremes however (which is probably where you are) women's finances are quite healthy. According to one report, women will be the main breadwinners in three out of four families by 2010. According to another report, women in the 18-24 age group are more likely to be employed in the future than men.

Despite the undoubted gender shift, a matching change in female attitudes to money seems to be on time-delay. In some quarters, the early nineties' slogan of "Women are just as good as men" has sneakily reverted to "Women should get men to pay for everything". That doesn't mean though that all women can be dismissed as money-grabbers.

High-salaried women often lament that it's hard to find men

who aren't threatened by the amount they earn. There's a great deal of truth here, although we don't completely buy this argument. Money is a form of power and any increase in earnings will naturally increase expectations, as it does for middle-aged male pop stars. The real problem is not, in our observation, the money; it is that women are already more choosy than men so . . . *so* don't be fooled by media tales of Lady Muck marrying the gardener. These stories stand out because they are rare and there are nearly always additional factors, such as age-linked insecurity, or obsessive physical attraction, that underlie them.

If she has her short-term glasses on, no woman is out of your league. Long term, however, a high-earning woman does not want a man who will detract, or worse, extract from her income. At the other extreme, a low-income woman will prefer a man who can take her out of the poverty trap. Money still matters, and it's useless to pretend otherwise. For those men who sweat at the thought of triple-figure restaurant bills, don't despair. You can overcome your spending limitations by showing a monetary mentality that women will respect. This does not necessarily involve paying for the drinks when you first meet her, but it does involve not asking her consistently to pay for your drinks. Later on, you can show her that though you may not have much money, you are willing to spend it on her and her alone.

Status
Music and film celebrities have always been aware of status, and now male strippers have joined the fame-game. Put simply, the man who is attractive to women is attractive to even more women. It is true that both men and women bask in reflected glory if their partner is obviously desirable, but this is not a chicken and egg situation. Men can switch off the opinions of others more easily than they can switch off libido, so it's clear that self-satisfaction is where true male motivation usually lies.

Women are not sheep either, but, when her hen-night pals

shriek at the sight of a stripper's bare torso, any passionate woman will want him too. Why not? He has already passed the most stringent test of partner potential – vetting by other women.

Out in the street, the only men who have comparable instant status, apart from especially handsome men, are those who have partners, those with intriguing sexual reputations (step forward the dark-eyed Latin lovers) and those with authoritative jobs. It is common for younger men without any of these attributes to try and put-down other men as a way of boosting their status. There's no need for this. So doing reflects badly on the perpetrator anyway.

All you need is to realise the value of showing women you are comfortable with other women.

Any man who is seen holding a conversation with another woman, for example, has immediate status. Besides, there is another aspect of status which, in the due course of time, all men have on their side. Age. Age is still a reliable indicator of wealth. Also, the evolutionary scientists argue that, as men retain their reproductive powers longer, the attractive power of male good looks does not decline with the years in quite the same way as once powerful feminine attractiveness may wear thin. Even if you can't reconcile any wrinkles of your own with this theory of facial smoothness, there is no doubt that age is also a conscious sign of maturity. Since more divorcing women are nowadays citing unreasonable behaviour as grounds, you can take comfort that any such sign of emotional control will increase attraction. As for our wrinkle-free readers – well, your attraction is obvious!

Looks

At ground level, there are only two sorts of man who can disregard most of this book and still succeed with women. The first is the man who has lived the text. The second is the man who is handsome. A famous man means nothing to a woman who doesn't know him; a rich man must show his wealth; a handsome man only has to show his face. The confident woman who approaches the tanned Adonis in a deafening night club is not responding to personality. And she may give him every contact number she's got, even if he's boring.

Generally, women don't like to admit the importance of looks. Such an admission might make them look shallow and basic . . . "just like men". However, scientists are now discovering that sight may be the primary relationship sense, for both sexes. Tests have shown that even babies react more to pretty faces. The best suggestion why good looks should matter so much to a woman is that they are a physical statement of invisible genetic quality – a potent biological magnet that works on her desire to have a healthy child. Women may not drool over stunners as might men (certainly not when men are around) but what they see will always count.

At this point, some men may wonder why we are hammering the nails in the coffin, so far as any plain – or even ugly – contemporary of theirs is concerned. Likewise, any woman reading the above might regard our views on good looks (in private at least) as crushingly banal. Have they been inserted because of the authors' insecurities about the facially fortunate? Nice try, but we're covered here. One of your authors is blessed with a highly defined bone structure, another has been known to produce the exclamation-mark look of interest from women more than once, while the third . . . well, the unfortunate view is that his face could break a mirror! It doesn't stop him succeeding though, because he realised he'd been whacked with the ugly stick from an early age, and has had time to adjust.

Rather, our assertions about looks are aimed at a small number of men who may not accept how important they are. Those males who seem to cling so desperately to the belief that personality is the most powerful initial tool of attraction will therefore indulge in the most self-destructive of all pursuits: namely – competing for women against men physically equipped to be more successful.

It can be a painful proposition to accept at first but the

realities are that some men will form more relationships than you just by virtue of their biological advantage. This doesn't make them "better" than you, just luckier.

Honestly, there's no need to smash the bathroom mirror – even if it's only your mother who thinks you're good looking. Never forget that, in the same way that rich men are paranoid about gold-diggers, good looks come complete with inevitable disadvantages that men with unremarkable features can easily avoid. Consider the following:

Handsome men

* Like attractive women, they have no control over whom they attract.
* Are often accused of leading women on, regardless of no such intention.
* Find that women will try harder to disguise the nastier aspects of their characters. This is no help when you start to discover that many relationships break down once the novelty of capture wears off and women allow their true personalities to come through.
* Handle rejection badly, simply because they're less used to it.
* Don't have a natural incentive to develop their personalities. The Himbo is as much a stereotype as the Bimbo.
* Have a reputation among women for selfishness and ill treatment.
* Worry more about their good looks as they have so much more to lose.
* Are sometimes isolated by the less handsome male majority.

Plain men

* Find it easier to challenge female assumptions because less is expected of them.

* Find that women care less about disguising their personalities. This helps plain men make more accurate partner choices.
* Can flirt with abandon.
* Have all the incentive to develop their personalities.
* Other men may dislike you but your looks (something you can't change) won't cause resentment.
* Have a reputation for doing more to please.
* May unfortunately have met with female rejection, but gained from the experience.
* Will find in Chapter 2 how paying attention to plain looks can only improve them (without resorting to surgical nips and tucks).

Plain men can also benefit from an ''X'' factor of association that seems to have little to do with biology. One passionate experience with a man of a certain look or background can, it seems, hook a woman onto that type for life. There's only so much experimenting she can do and, if she's had a good time once, she may return for more of the same. Without you knowing it, other young men may have done you an enormous favour.

Early on, we talked about women's desire for making ''accurate'' choices. Now we can define their self-imposed choosiness in terms of intuition or perhaps just a knack for spotting potential: be it genetic (for passing on to offspring), fathering ability (to make both the life of her and any children easier) or partner-potential (ability to make her feel good). However you may regard such feminine skill, you must always allow the superficials their due in a woman's choice because they *naturally* aid accuracy. These attributes can all be conveyed silently, without any of the deception that can be involved when men talk to women.

This makes superficials, initially at least, more powerful
    traction than personality. Knowing this is all part of
    picture. You have to accept that all your circum-
    vill affect the way a woman reacts to you. Clothes,

shoes, hairstyle, race, age, accent, height, looks – in the time it takes for her to turn away after catching your eye, she will have used everything she saw and heard to form an opinion of you and what you can do for her. Pre-conversation, such opinions tend to be as fixed as the circumstances themselves but always bear in mind you can change a woman's mind by talking with her.

If you are long on the superficials, you may well need to control those inner fears about being wanted for what you have, not who you are. It is only wise to avoid women who are heavily materialistic but, like it or not, the superficials are a valid part of your attraction.

If you don't have them, then you can certainly stop taking instant rejection as such an affront to your personality. A woman's assumptions about these material factors are largely outside your control. You only need to worry about the times when a desirable woman responds positively to you and yet you fail to capitalise.

INSECURITIES

As a collective whole, women have never had so much power and, quite frankly, some have overdosed. But how, exactly, does modern man control the creeping feelings of inadequacy *he* may have, when so much current evidence points to the intimate dice being loaded in favour of women?

Understanding that she has the same basic worries as you will lessen the fear you have of an individual woman.

For example, how many times have you talked to a woman, run out of things to say and then thought it was your fault that the conversation didn't continue further? What makes you think the same worry about being boring didn't go through her mind too? It may interest men to know that they aren't the only ones, either, who sometimes go home thinking that they blew it by being too clever or talking too much about themselves.

A woman may have other, more pressing worries concerning relationships. Experience may have taught her that assumptions can be proven painfully wrong; trust is often misplaced; game-playing can have dangerous consequences; expectations can go unfulfilled; competition is stressful; arrogance makes rejection more painful; intensive careers can affect relationships; independence can be lonely, yet hard to give up; and then there are the touchy areas of age and looks.

The fiercest feminist rhetoric won't change the facts that men prefer women who are young and pretty or that there are plenty of women who consider themselves to be neither. Add emotional sensitivity, cultural restrictions and anxieties about sexual needs and you realise the other half of the human race is likely to feel just as insecure as may you, if not more so. All this and we haven't yet even dealt with the biggest insecurity of all – guilt.

Guilt

All women have to contend with guilty feelings sometimes. However, within the broad range of wanting it all and not wanting much, some women manage to feel guilty on account of almost everything about their relationships. These ladies torture themselves with guilt for anything that can be construed as unethical such as: rejecting nice guys, staying at home with the kids rather than joining the rat race, treading on others' toes to get ahead, having sexual double standards, being a dependent-independent, putting on fronts, shifting the blame onto men, and wishing evil on their best friend's relationship with a wonderful new boyfriend.

Why women can sometimes be so burdened with guilt is not clear. Perhaps the guilt is genetically driven as some researchers (the same branch who feel the urge for conformity is inborn) have speculated. Even if this is not so, it is certainly true that having a healthy and clear conscience is a major asset to motherhood. The onus has always been on women to rear children so perhaps this also explains why nine out of ten lone parents left to bring up their children single-handed are women.

The origins of guilt may remain impenetrable, but you must give it due consideration. Rogues do this naturally. Natural-born rascals seem to attract women *precisely because* they have that guilt-free disregard for consequences that so many women wish they themselves had. Not only do they attract women, but rogues forge relationships of perplexing length, chiefly, we reckon, because their bad-boy behaviour auto-matically transfers the moral power to the women with whom they become involved. Remember our premise on compatibil-ity (page 20). Women never lose sight of their own needs in affairs of the heart! This doesn't mean you have to behave recklessly so as to ease a woman's guilt or make her feel more secure about anything else! Rogues may lead charmed lives (to the point of disbelief!) but in the long run they get unanimously dumped. Why? Because they are exceptionally selfish and in reality everything, even a woman they actually like, comes as secondary to their own gratification. When a rogue lies to a woman that she is his very reason for being and then tests the bed springs with her best friend, who can blame her for wanting to jettison such baggage?

It isn't easy consistently to put a woman's needs first, but you must avoid the needless mistakes of overloading her insecurities through selfishness or neglect. The foul tide of popular opinion may seem to be that women prefer men that treat them badly, but the truth is that genuine, deep-down kindness, *such as not abusing your knowledge about women's worries*, will never go out of fashion. You will need to give a woman reassurance, without patronising her, should you feel she really needs it.

Her:	. . . my sister's just had a baby. Sometimes I wonder if I should take time off to have children or carry on with my career . . .
Negative:	How old did you say you were again? Thirty? If I were you, I'd hurry up, before it's too late.
Positive:	Well, you're only thirty. I thought that was the average age for mothers these days.

Her:	I live in a two-bed, but I'm going to have to move soon. My flatmate's got a new man and they're all lovey-dovey.
Negative:	How come she's got someone and you haven't? Is she better-looking than you?
Positive:	I understand how things like that make sharing tough. Any chance of getting a place on your own?

Also, and this can be harder to come to terms with, you must accept that many women still believe they get the toe-end of society. Rightly or wrongly, or during periods of stress, these women feel so weighed down with worries that, when you first meet, they really won't want to know about yours. Especially not if they are moans about ex-partners, mothers or female empowerment! So keep them to yourself until the time is right to share. This may be after five minutes, or after five months; however, if she makes you feel you can *never* show vulnerability, beware. Your interests may not be her prime concern . . .

2

THE WAY YOU ARE

Looks, status and fortune all have a disadvantage. They are merely one-way triggers of a woman's emotions. Only personality, brought out in two-way conversation, can fully engage a woman by both stimulating her and by showing her that she too is stimulating. You may not previously have thought of your personality as the most powerful arouser of a woman's emotions but please be assured that it is the most *essential* factor that can encourage her to respond.

Just the thought of trying to open a conversation with (never at) a woman is enough to make some grown men shake, but it's not as tough as it sounds. Having the insight to approach an unhappy gooseberry can do the trick, as can simply listening to what a woman has to say.

Success naturally relies on confidence, which is why so many men (mistakenly) try to fake having it. True confidence, which makes you attractive to all women, must come from within. Confidence which shows (without showing off) springs from knowledge, like that given in the last chapter about the intimate world around you, as well as from what you should be able to absorb from this chapter about developing your intimate potential – all combined with common sense and good observation.

CONTROL

The oldest profession relies on a negative answer to an equally ancient question: can men control lust? Homer didn't think so when he wrote about Odysseus and the sirens; Samson wished he had more than physical strength once Delilah sheared him like a sheep; and if only cigar boxes in the Oval office could talk . . . The historical solution to all this real and mythical lust was thought to be simple: control your women.

We say "no" to that! As far as we are concerned, the cultural concept of men in charge of women is little more than sexist compensation for the desire differences. Men may be stronger than women, more competitive and they may have different skills, but that does not make male domination an inevitable consequence of biology.

In truth, human nature simply does not reward suppression in relationships. Men gain most from women when women are happy. Put-down (as opposed to protected) women are likely to leave, not laugh.

Nonetheless we do live in the real world, and we do accept that it can be difficult to dismiss mythical (and mistaken) ideas of male supremacy where relationships are concerned. Nature *has* left men with advantages, but try persuading a 25 year old, low-income, virgin man of that! Suggest that he stifle any domineering tendencies either because his reproductive powers will last almost twice as long as his female counterpart's, or because potential girlfriends are (slightly) less geared to choosing partners on the basis of youth and beauty, or because he is likely to be better at chess and yo-yo tricks than most women, and you are unlikely to succeed. Partly this is because his female contemporaries seem so determined to rub his face in *their* new-found freedom of choice. Yet the truth is, the choice has always been theirs.

If your love life is going to get anywhere at all you *must* accept that you cannot control any woman. If she wants to go for a man that you've told her will treat her badly, she will; if she wants to go for your friend even though it's you who has spent hours talking to her, you can't stop her; if she wants to disrupt your carefully thought-out plan of seduction by cancelling at the last minute, it's really out of your hands. You can't force her to do anything she doesn't want to do.

You can only hope to *influence* her.

How do you influence a woman? Always look towards respect and friendship. Neither aspect may be quite enough on its own but, together, these ingredients are the very stuff of – dare we say it – love. A woman may respect her tyrant of a male boss but she won't want to drink with him. She may like her amiable work colleague but, if he doesn't pull his weight, she'll tear into him in a way she'd never dream of doing with the boss.

If we had to choose we'd plump (just) for friendship. Genuine friendship is closer to love than respect will ever be. When she likes you, it's amazing how much else falls into place. A receding hairline becomes a sign of maturity not aging, a paunch becomes a sign of good living rather than sloth and a moon face is seen as cute, not effeminate!

An almost essential component of such friendship is an ability to overrule the animosity that a persistent concept of male dominance (patriarchy) can create. Even young women are hyper-sensitive to the man who holds the slightest gender-grudge and there really is no long-term way to hide such an attitude of superiority. Smother such thoughts at birth, or they will always hamper your relations with women. Luckily, however badly you may feel that you've been treated by women in the past, however much stress you reckon certain women give you, however unfair you feel society is to men like you, it will only take one good relationship to change your perspective. The female race as a whole is not your enemy; ignorance may be.

Caution: handle with care

This enlightened attitude is something you show, rather than speak about. Women are so used to male chauvinism that the man who "preaches" equality can make them suspicious, and even annoyed. They know the way the world really works and they don't need a man to tell them otherwise. Say that you would work just as hard for a woman boss who was good at her job but never say that you think women make better bosses than men – even if you believe the latter.

We hope we have convinced you that a control-freak attitude to women is obsolete. What gains respect is being in control of yourself. Don't worry, this doesn't mean adopting monastic practices of self-denial. Just stick to doing the simple things within the remit of every man, like not talking about sex until women do, not pandering to a beautiful tease, not wasting time and energy plotting the downfall of men who are more successful than you, and not allowing others to dictate your choice of partner.

COMPETITION

As you may have guessed, we are not great advocates of competition for women. Not, you understand, that we are complete wimps. Sure, you must be prepared for the fact that a woman will always compare you to other men. Plus, tales are legion of how having a combative edge can make the difference between gold and silver, or profit and bankruptcy. We also acknowledge how competition has benefited society. Necessity may be the mother of invention, but a blood test would surely prove competition to be the estranged father.

However, direct competition for women is not as straightforward as a race, be it on athletics tracks or to build a high flying company on the stock market. Not only does a woman rate you on a point-scoring basis, not only does such competition often degenerate into spectacles as pathetic as two bald men fighting over a comb; there are no fall-back compensations of a second-place award or increased market share even if you don't win. The relationship loser gets nothing. That's when things can turn really ugly and, as usual, it's women that suffer.

Unfortunately, it seems that more and more men don't care about women's suffering. There is an increasing tendency to believe that selfishness is the core of human nature and that, when dating, any method of seduction is justified if the result is sex. This reasoning is not just due to some relic of patriarchy. Unwittingly perhaps, the popularisation of science has fuelled this twisted thinking. All people hear from that quarter is talk of selfish genes, opposing sexual strategies and conflict. Actually, any evolutionary text worth its salt will take pains to point out the prevalence of co-operation as well as competition. However, this news is not as "sexy" as competitive biology and therefore it never seems to be so widely quoted.

With this general background, the notion that jealousy and competition are inborn and undeniable would appear to hold sway. But have you also come across the proposition of "game theory", which, linked to conformity, suggests that co-operation is likewise a natural instinct, instead of the construct of "civilised" society which it is so often deemed to be? Life may well be about survival of the fittest, but the ability to get along with others is as much a part of that fitness as defensive reflexes are to the champion boxer. This matches the emotional truism that ordinary people have never needed scientists to spell out: namely that men and women *both* need to be needed.

Who or what is going to fulfil this requirement for single women nowadays? Other girls? Now that women are so openly competitive, the concept of sisterhood is getting more ragged by the day. Casual sex? Well, the thrill of sex can scarcely balance the constant threat of disease, damage to reputation and the subliminal dangers involved in high-handedly rejecting men before they're ready to go. Will money do it? To an extent yes. Wealth gives women a certain amount of freedom and pleasure. But two incomes are better than one, and most women don't have access to enough of the filthy lucre to buy away their troubles. What about children? Of course they fulfil a need but she may not want them now. Children can't fulfil every need and, regardless of how relationships develop, most mothers do not start out intending to bring up their children alone. The answer, even though she may not want to admit it, remains men. However, if men are going to keep giving her the hassle, the hurt, the chauvinism that so often comes with go-getting natures, she'd rather stay single. What she actually wants, more and more, is the man who sees a relationship as a partnership not as a competition.

The third and final reason for developing a non-competitive approach, at least where women are concerned, is (please forgive us!) an assumptive one. Frankly, the one characteristic that all men reading this book will have in common is not shyness, lack of superficials or problems with giving; it's lack of the ability to compete with other men for women without presenting an over-competitive or even hostile aura that swiftly turns any woman off. Even those with a healthy dose of drive, such as the successful businessman, may nonetheless feel unnecessarily anxious next to the jobseeker with film star looks, leading to subtle changes in behaviour easily spotted by women.

How do you genuinely subdue your competitive urges? Well, they do seem to be instinctive so there's no point in trying to eradicate them completely from your persona. Besides, you need your natural style for success in other areas of life. As with any desire you have to control, it may be best to harness your drive and turn it inwards. Though it may not be easy, we suggest this so that you choose in the future to compete less with the other guys and more, for example, with such things as your own fears or female assumptions. The main strategy should always be getting women directly interested in you, rather than in any way trying to rely on other men to make you look interesting.

Make sure you avoid any sting or hurt creeping into your words or actions; if competition from another man is clouding your relationship to the extent that you cannot curb your annoyance, you can be pretty sure you will never win anyway.

Jealousy

When a woman wants a man, probably the only thing that will end her desire is that man himself. If you're not romantically involved, forget about trying to divert her from him with negative tales of your rival's dishonesty, sexuality or bank balance. She will listen to every word you say, but all she will hear is the thumping bass of your jealousy. Outside of intimacy, women do not respect this emotion, as it too easily suggests that the man who displays it has a controlling nature. Let her desire run to its natural end.

Compare realistically

Your past, personality, physique and present all make you a unique human being. The same applies to everyone else. You need to bear this in mind in order to stop exploding with envy when others, especially friends, are more successful than you. Ask yourself:

Is he more handsome than you? (Be honest!)

Is he taller than you?

Does he have more money?

Does he socialise more often?

Has he had more girlfriends than you?

Was his upbringing less restricted than yours?

Every yes is a reason why he may have more confidence with women than you. If you answer no to all the above, and the man in question still attracts more women than you, stick with him. You can learn much from this guy. And for free!

Couples

When you're single they're everywhere you look but being paired up doesn't necessarily make them happier than you are. Dare we suggest that most people have no idea how many other people – male and female – are prepared to stay in destructive relationships rather than face the fear of single-dom? Couples often have an unspoken agreement to present a united front in public. So you may never see the private truth. Have you ever wondered how many of your partnered friends also secretly respect the fact that you've kept your sanity all the time you've been alone?

Self-interest

Having a conscience makes you a worthwhile human being. However, just as you may have a problem with competition, you may also have a problem with putting your own feelings first. If so, it may be time you recognised the rarity of real altruism. How much of the male desire to bring a woman to orgasm is linked to his own ego and how much to her pleasure? Provided both parties benefit, does it really matter? You must decide. Unnecessary feelings of guilt can prevent romance from flowering. Women *do* turn away from out-and-out rogues but neither do they like men consumed by guilt that apparently defies logic.

   You must come to terms with genuine remorse but being cluttered with undeserved guilt merely hampers you from giving the essentials to promote a relationship – such as flattery and reassurance. You also need self-interest for those times when it is necessary to depart (only slightly) from a strictly ethical route. Thus you should: choose a one-to-one date rather than a group arrangement, thereby keeping your new love-interest away from your more successful friends until the relationship has been cemented; allow time to realise the benefits of showing her you are comfortable with other women; always prefer to give most to those women who respect you, rather than succumb to that old (Groucho) Marxism, ''Why should I want to belong to any club that would have me as a member?''

Piety

Depending on your outlook, you may see the lack of short-term sex, associated with being a less competitive man, as a problem. Instead, you should consider the advantages. Nice guys have the widest appeal of any male type, move into the friendship zone faster than anyone else and naturally repel many women who cause problematic relationships. There may well be immediate friction between you and headstrong women who don't have social boundaries of behaviour, yet still feel guilty about the way they act; inflexible women who stubbornly believe all men are the morally inferior sex; women who prefer to go for "unavailable" men and those women who see criminal sentences as a sign of kudos. But this is all good. However, you do have to be careful not to blind the remaining desirable women with the shine of your halo. Humanise yourself by not preaching, not judging aloud, and by letting people know about some (censored) mistakes you have made.

EXPECTATIONS

A strange twist of male and female nature is that the most unsuccessful romantics are often the choosiest. Women may find it harder to buck their biological instincts of choice, but you may have to reduce yours in order even to enter into a happy relationship, which may then develop. Only those men who are constantly approached by women can truly afford to be too choosy!

Never paint yourself into a corner with public declarations of your high partner standards or by being derisive of other men's choices.

Choice-affecters

Lessen the amount of time you spend around those people who restrict your freedom of choice. It is out of order (mostly) for anyone to list reasons why a girl isn't right for you, and in any event whoever does so is probably just a control freak. Many choice-affecters are women (relatives, female friends) and they often have vested reasons for influencing your choice, perhaps for trying to apply *their* standards to your life.

Reasons can be that simple or more convoluted. For example, some female friends may have featured you as the male lead in one or two of their erotic dreams, but they have long ago decided that they are not going to make a pass at you. If they can keep you single, keep other women from wanting you, it validates their decisions not to go for you. This is oddly flattering and can lead somewhere if you have the guts to make an issue out of it.

You: Why do you interrupt me every time I talk to another girl? Are you interested in me?

Her: No way! Don't be so sensitive, I'm just having a laugh.

You: Pity. If you had said yes it might change the way I feel about you. But since you're doing it for a laugh, please stop. I don't like being single and I'd hate for you to come between me and a woman I really like.

Without embarrassing yourself, you've let her know how you feel. She may even take you up on the hint of attraction, although it's more likely she will be wary of blocking you again, and that is the main objective.

Sexpectations
Everybody's at it but you, right? Wrong! You can forget the lurid tales from Sunday tabloids of sex scandals involving rich business tycoons, the torrid affairs of political bigwigs and the lifestyle titillation of men's and women's magazines. Every bachelor has a sexual drought and the results of three comprehensive British surveys, each having over 15,000 respondents, bear testimony to this. The stark conclusions are that, apart from a happy few, regular sex and single men are mutually exclusive terms. True, sexual surveys are notoriously unreliable but, given the current culture of success, there is no reason for men to own up to inactive sex lives unless they're being honest. Remember any first-night intimacy you do get is more likely to be vertical, not horizontal. Bearing in mind that casual sex is synonymous with sexual disease, that's not such a bad thing.

CHARM
If you want a girl you can take home to meet mother, you won't find her by treating women like sex objects. On the

other hand, you have to recognise that women are sexual beings too. Only charm can bridge this gap. It tells a woman, in the nicest possible way, that you want to be more than friends with her. How? With simple reassurance:

"Don't worry. Your curves are in all the right places" (said with a big grin)

and flattery,

"Your looks made me come over, but it's your personality that's making it hard to leave"

but, mostly, charm is about bodytalk. The lavish ceremonies at Cannes and Hollywood do little more than celebrate those who have finest control over their gestures. You may never win an Oscar, but it won't hurt to be positive with your body.

Smile
A simple smile is a universally friendly gesture, infectious and free. Practise a warm smile; neither hold it too long nor drop it too quickly. Practise for those inevitable times when you aren't in the best of moods but still have the urge to talk to a desirable woman. You may feel fraudulent, but transmit bad vibes and you are likely to get them back. Beware, though, of becoming a Cheshire cat; drop your smile according to the situation, like when she tells you that her pet canary has just dropped off its perch.

Eyes
Eye contact is the premier way that most women signal their choice. It is less risky for them. That's why women will usually always respect a man with "good eyes", who silently conveys his own interest in them. Women nonetheless know that it's not good manners to stare, and women are the better mannered sex. However, even the shy woman who

is interested will not shun your eyeline totally, although she may try to avoid talking.

Moderating the amount of eye contact is important. Too much and you risk making her nervous, too little and you look shifty. Look away from time to time as this shows you are thinking intently. Equally, if you use lots of eye contact when listening, this shows that you are attentive and interested. Try not to look around when she is talking, as this shows lack of commitment.

Always look her in the eye when you make an important point.

Touch and space

Most men possess an intuitive idea that touching strangers is not appropriate behaviour in British culture. Unfortunately, rather fewer men seem fully able to respect personal space. When you first meet, you need go only as close as is necessary for her to hear you, given the background noise of your environment. She will then dictate how close she is willing to let you get. If she makes a (possibly) negative initial move, such as leaning away, moving backwards, crossing her arms or legs or twisting her body side-on, respect this. Women often back off to a distance with which they feel comfortable when they are first approached. If she does this, don't fret. Just follow her with your eyes – not your body. So long as she's prepared to keep talking, there's a chance she'll come closer.

Defence

Avoid defensive gestures. They can indicate you're uncomfortable and lack confidence. The main defensive gestures are the armfold, clenched hands and features, and shifty eyes. Practise control by deliberately testing yourself, initiating conversations – especially where you already know the lady to be easily slighted. Consciously stop yourself from displaying defence. Use open gestures, such as upturned palms and partly outstretched arms to display honesty and friendliness.

Positivity

Speaking positively is a key way quiet men can appeal to a girl's desire for a confident man. Upbeat bodytalk should always be matched by words. Avoid can't, don't, won't, shouldn't, couldn't, wouldn't; choose can, will, great, I'm up for that, etc.

CAUTION: HANDLE WITH CARE

Never brag about feeling confident. So doing can make her suspect the reverse – that you lack confidence.

Flattery

Unsolicited touching is perhaps the main difference between smarm and charm but ill-timed, excessive flattery comes a close second. The creep, desperate for one thing only, swamps a woman with empty flattery. The charmer, no less keen, is careful not to make the same error. He will gear his flattery to the woman concerned, time it when he thinks she wants to hear it, once he feels that she respects his opinion, and space it out to greatest effect.

Her:	I hate my hands; they're so wrinkled.
Creep:	They're beautiful; you can put them on me if you like.
Charmer:	Everyone has a part of their body they don't like. From where I'm standing, you've got so much else with which to be happy.

Smarmy men are the reason flattery gets an unfairly bad press. Whatever you may think, however, modern girls are not yet so sophisticated that they refuse to be a little won over by flattery.

For example, common sense dictates men should lie if necessary when women request opinions on body mass. You don't have to lie if you find her plus points. Simply avoid the minus signs.

"You really do look young. You've got no wrinkles." (So, no need to mention that she's slightly overweight.)

"You've got superb clear skin." (Keep to yourself that her hairstyle doesn't suit her.)

"You've got a great body. How do you keep yourself in such fine shape?" (Silence your feeling that she's really quite plain.)

"You've got lovely blue eyes." (Always get the eye colour right! This helps avoid mention of her big nose!)

Two powerful mental sweeteners that can be used whenever there is a hint of truth are: (1) to tell younger women that they seem mature beyond their years and (2) to compliment a beautiful woman on her personality as well as her looks.

APPEARANCE
No woman ever turned down a man on the grounds that he was clean and tidy. Working on posture and physique will also increase your chances of success.

Hygiene
You may think you smell like roses, but it may just be that you lack friends with the courage to tell you the truth. Don't wait until you start receiving anonymous packages of soap in your in-tray. Start practising overall personal hygiene if you don't already. Shower once a day, and use deodorant. Aftershave is extra, but it is worthwhile investing in a good quality musk rather than cheap skin-stripper. Try out a few fragrances and see which smells best ten minutes after it has been applied. Your feet may seem a long way down but don't forget they can become very smelly.

Wash outer garments at least once a week (more frequently if you're a heavy smoker) and don't wait until your underwear starts sticking to your skin before you change it. Use mouthwash and oral hygiene in addition to the standard, twice-a-day, 45 degree toothbrushing routine that keeps dentist appointments short. Seek medical/dental help if you're inclined to have bad breath.

Clothes and looks
You don't have to dress like a male model to attract women but at a time when so many magazines are entirely devoted to

fashion you've got to make some effort. Try to avoid these turn-offs: worn clothes (particularly jeans); unfashionably short trousers; scruffy stubble growth; battered shoewear; untidy hairstyles; un-ironed clothing.

Women have suggested to us that a man who is overdressed can also be unattractive. The implied vanity can be off-putting, a role-reversal of the feelings men get with women who dress too flashily. It is important to wear the right clothes for the right occasion.

Body
If you can, improve your physical fitness. If you are healthy, there's nothing but time to stop you from adopting a keep-fit programme. An hour out of your week won't kill you. The benefits of exercise are so well known there's no need to bore you with them here. It may help if you have certain incentives to exercise. For example, there are likely to be more women at an aerobics course than following a bodybuilding programme.

Posture
Avoid slumping and slouching as this looks negative and lazy. Try to keep your posture upright, chest out and shoulders relaxed but back. This increases stature and expresses confidence. The same goes for walking. Keep your head and neck upright, chest out and your eyes ahead. Putting a smile on your face puts one on your life too!

INSIGHT
Insight helps you join the dots between what women say and what they really mean. The best way to develop insight is to realise that while "Naff off and leave me alone!" will tell you everything you need to know, very few outward signs can be taken in isolation. To some women, for example, swearing is as natural as breathing and, just because they throw choice language at you, it doesn't mean they are trying to hurt.

Normally, signs of attraction (or even of dislike) come in a *clustered* trio of body, word and timing. The most important method as between men and women is undoubtedly body talk, but you shouldn't try to turn body language into an exact science. Keep it simple. Concentrate on eyes, touch, space, body position and facial expression. Be warned. Women do not like being sized up like prize cattle. Scan with discretion, speed and accuracy. The quicker you can evaluate her mind-set, the better; you'll move faster than other men, or avoid wasting time and energy approaching someone likely to reject you.

You can practise scanning anywhere, but it's often best done in the company of total strangers, for example on bus or train journeys. This way you have fewer pre-conceptions and your first impressions count more. Look away towards a fixed point rather than at any one person, and try and form images of the people around you. What moods are they in? What do they each really look like? What do you think of their individual circumstances or body postures? Do you think the hard-looking woman to your left is genuinely hostile or just putting on a defensive front? Does the woman just on the periphery of your vision look worth talking to or not? Is she looking at you? After a few moments studying these images in your mind's eye, you can casually turn to see how your impressions match up to reality – all without staring or risk of embarrassment.

After a while (provided you are not too fussy), you'll be able to select out those women likely to be companionable for you with exocet accuracy.

CAUTION: HANDLE WITH CARE
Resist ever showing off by indulging in public "psycho-analysis" of how clever you are. Women may fear and will hate a knowing man who thinks aloud, especially if he's right! If you know so much, why are you still single? Empathise, never analyse.

Careless: I can tell you don't agree with me because you've folded your arms. You might not know it, but that's a defensive gesture.

Careful: Something tells me you don't agree with me?

HONESTY

How can a woman *not* appreciate honesty? It's the one thing that lets her know where she stands. And if you are honest with tact and diplomacy, she will appreciate you even more.

So how can you, a lying, cheating, despicable, reprobate (don't take it personally, it's an occupational hazard of being male!) become more genuine towards women? By force of habit and by being honest as a matter of principle.

Honesty should pose no difficulty the first time you meet a woman. If currently committed to another girlfriend (or would like to be but are yet unsure of her feelings) you can simply show interest without in any way raising hope. That will keep good vibes under control and command much respect too.

But how *do* you "make a pass" at her when you *are* free to do so?

Certain thoughts now need your most urgent inner appraisal; we will run through them in detail in a moment:

Am I prepared to let her know that I like her?

Am I prepared to commit?

Am I prepared to let her know how long-term my interest will be?

Am I prepared *not* to adjust too much?

Am I prepared *not* to tell her everything?

Am I prepared to continue along these lines with her indefinitely?

Am I prepared to let her know that I like her?

The best encounters are those where everything is so touchy-feely positive that saying how much you like her seems superfluous. Usually though, intentions need to be openly stated and you can't expect her necessarily to bear this responsibility. Taking verbal chances is what separates the men from the pre-pubescent. There is simply no magic formula which will remove the absolute necessity of your putting your ego on the line. You must bring up the subject of how keen you are at some point. You can try and calculate the risk, but even the bookmakers lose out sometimes. You might get rejected. So what? If you're not prepared to give something of yourself to women, their doubts about age, looks and relationship potential (or almost anything else!) will always make them uncertain about the strength of your interest, and, most often, you will lose out.

The calculation is in the timing and while there will never be a perfect time, the following situations offer your best chances of success:

* Try to "put your cards on the table" on a face-to-face, one-to-one occasion.
* Try when she seems in a good mood. Some men mistakenly choose a moment when she's vulnerable or distressed. The danger is that a woman may feel subsequently that you were just trying to take advantage. Later on, she might remember your pass positively when she is vulnerable but may well disregard it altogether when her mood improves.
* If suitable music is playing, always try and dance with her. This will give you a good insight into how receptive she will be to your move.
* Do so when *she* has asked you to meet up with her.
* Wait for a time when her cluster signs (see above) are favourable.
* If it's a new encounter, ALWAYS ASK FOR A CONTACT NUMBER BEFORE SHE LEAVES!! (Modesty may stop *her* calling you, even if she likes you.)

What should you say? Well, you don't always have to promise eternal devotion. All women have too much self-respect to fall for a sex-mad hound, but overly intense romantic statements can also easily raise a woman's barriers – particularly single, career girls. However you put what you feel into words, you must always be whole-hearted, nonetheless. Try to put aside any negative thoughts (they have a habit of resolving themselves anyway) and to capture in what you say those things that attract you most about her. This helps your emotions turn into words that will come across sincerely, positively.

Don't start with "I wonder...?" or "Are you feeling...?" Such beginnings irritate, unlike confident openings, "Will you join me...?" or "You're the best..." which captivate. There is always the fear that she may ridicule your desire however you express it, but most women are hugely diplomatic once you let them know that they mean something to you.

Am I prepared to commit?

The length of your commitment in your thoughts will depend on many variables, but at the barest minimum you should be ready to keep talking to her, despite perhaps the presence of her more attractive friends!

Am I prepared to let her know how long-term my interests will be?

This is where the real problems start! Our ears have singed with the complaints of women who say the honest man is as rare as a dodo feather, but this is unduly harsh. The more likely truth is that women fight so shy of revealing interest – even very strong interest – that men sometimes feel they have to go a bit "overboard". Ergo, men promise the earth, and this can have dire consequences when those promises aren't kept. There is always the likelihood of pain when friendship and intimacy do not develop from the short to long-term, but an improved level of insight can reduce your chances of getting into that situation. Try to make sure you really do have a good idea what wavelength she's on, and never talk directly about full-on commitment if that is not your aim.

Insofar as the latter goes, we take a leaf out of women's books. All three of us have ended up hurt at least once by failing to recognise the very private agendas of different women whom we were dating; hurt by women who, for whatever the real reason, did not want to continue a relationship.

Leaving aside morals or ethics for a moment, we should warn you that women's views about the right time to end a short-term relationship can vary between a goodnight peck on the cheek and "goodbye!" on the first date, to beyond spending nights together – whether or not you may have shared a bed.

Yes! Sometimes we felt used, but our joint conclusion has been that this was always as much our fault as theirs. With hindsight, we could see that the women concerned had, without exception, been very precise in their choice of attraction-speak. It was a case of "I really like you" not "I want to be with you for ever"; or "I want you" not "I want to spend the rest of my life with you". In our experience, her conscience can be relied upon to stop a woman from leading a man to think long-term when she isn't thinking that way herself.

We fully understand how you, too, may decide to avoid obvious statements of commitment, perhaps just for a while, until more water can pass under the bridge. You must then be prepared for her to whittle you down to that truth. She will want to be sure of your motives. She may share an interest more in fun and romance than in commitment, at least in the beginning. She may love sex; or may want to marry a virgin; but the thing to remember is that *truth* is the strongest ally you can both share, no matter what you each may desire from the relationship.

In time you may feel you want to consummate your relationship in sexual union. Your girlfriend may reach that same desire earlier or later, inside or outside of marriage, and so on. Let's assume you have already confirmed with *your-self* that *you* will feel comfortable with your decision, given your upbringing, religion, standards, values, and your resources and degree of commitment to any child were one to be born. Will she, likewise, feel comfortable? That is the key question upon which you MUST WAIT until you are sure you are both in agreement. That time may be now, never, or anywhere in between.

Here is one scenario you might meet:

You: I'm attracted to you.

Her: I know!

You: Well . . . I was thinking.

Her: What?

You: I'd like to take things further.

Her: How much further?

You: That you might like to come back to my place . . .

Her: For coffee?

You: I really hope you won't take this the wrong way, because I –

Her: Get to the point!

You: Well, it's more than that. I'd really like you to wake up next to me tomorrow.

Her: . . . supposing, and I'm just saying *supposing*, mind; supposing I did stay the night with you; then what?

You: I find you so sexy but I wouldn't want anything to happen that you might not be happy about once it did. I know I'm not ready for a total commitment, not now anyway.

You must now be mentally prepared to act and be content whatever she may reply.

CAUTION: HANDLE WITH CARE

This may demand being honest with yourself, apparently at a level beyond logic or reason but, accept her refusal (if it so be) you must.

We say *apparently* above, because of the profoundly differing sexual mores you may yourself hold sacrosanct, or meet, either in the society within which you live or some part of it, or perhaps in some other part of the world. Perhaps because it is such a strong deliverer of good judgment, sexual abstinence before marriage (i.e. from full sexual intercourse in the normal, procreative sense) has been a matter of contention among, for example, spiritual leaders, down the ages. Neither side of these arguments finds it easy to abide by the other's point of view. Each of us, however, must make our own choices and respect those of others. What needs saying here, too, is that those with stricter beliefs or interpretations need have no fear of "missing out"; there will always be plenty members of the opposite sex who are in tune with you. There is never any necessity to ditch your principles or your health concerns and deviate from conduct with which you know you can be happy in the aftermath. Neither you nor she need listen either to hearsay, heresy, or peer pressure, mischievous and misleading as these can often be.

Rogues, lads, ladettes and other short-term hedonists would pour scorn on all this advice. They would say that being candid simply means you ruin any chance of sex. They may be partly right, but so what? The reality is that not all women, either, will really appreciate the honesty involved in such comments. Some might even think you're a presumptuous prat. Fine. Let them. If you know a car is going to crash, you don't drive it, no matter what anyone else says.

By now, we hope you are fully aware of the importance of always giving proper due thought to the dating difficulties you may have to face, preparing yourself for the worst so your confidence isn't shattered if it happens. Luckily, however, almost by definition, the worst hardly ever happens and you won't find many women who would treat you in any callous sort of way. What you *will* find is that your integrity will always count for much more than you expect among women worthwhile chasing.

Am I prepared *not* to adjust too much?

There is an impulse in every man to gear his conversation according to the woman he's talking to and sometimes it can help. If she's down, cheer her up; if she's up, try and keep her there; and if she's out on a hen night, why bother with intense questions about the meaning of life? Still, you should only adjust so far. Leaving out obscure words so you don't make her feel small is fine. Affecting an accent so you can pretend to be on her level is not.

The more of the real you that attracts her, the longer it will last, but there is a less obvious reason to be as natural as possible. If she thinks you are disguising to impress, this will tip the power scales in her favour. Then you may have a problem taking her off that pedestal. Have faith in your newly-developing personality as being inherently attractive and avoid the following:

* Using slang you don't normally use.
* Using complex words you don't normally use.
* Trying to sound more intelligent than you are.
* Trying to sound a lot less intelligent than you are.
* Acting the extrovert. It's an attractive personality to adopt but never make promises you cannot keep. Otherwise you're always going to be under pressure to deliver.
* Playing the tough guy. Being Dirty Harry is a favourite fantasy of men who are gentle but this act will just attract the rough-loving type of woman.

Am I prepared *not* to tell her everything?

A contradiction, surely? Not quite. Women seldom expect men to tell the complete truth about everything (haven't you ever met a woman who lied about her age?) but they hate a bad liar. We don't advocate compulsive lying and heaven forbid you get caught up in the social epidemic of making out you're someone you're not, but there should always remain some mystery between you. *Total* honesty, then, may best be reserved a little for full relationships and those rare occasions when you click instantly. Otherwise, be content with telling her as much as you can bear her knowing. This is not so much lying as using common sense reticence. Consider, too, typical women's guile:

"You're a nice guy but . . ."

"I never date someone I work with."

"I'm happy being single."

"I'm too busy for a relationship."

"I haven't had many lovers."

"I have a boyfriend; he's abroad."

Again, we urge you to take women's ways on board. Never lie
to hurt or impress; save your minor fiblets only to protect both
your egos. Hopefully, you are aware of the need to protect her
ego. Work on protecting yours in three key areas too:

Money and status
It takes great strength to be open about your lack of funds once
you know the importance of money to relationships. We,
ourselves, to our own later regret, have not always managed to
be wholly truthful in the past. The best you can do is not go
overboard about your situation at first. Tell her the truth once a
relationship develops. If you are on a low income and conscious about it, however, you may choose initially lightly to
embellish your job description:

You say	In reality
I'm in Customer Services.	(Barman.)
I'm a Company Director.	(In family building firm.)
I'm a Produce Manager.	(Working on a fruit and veg stall.)
I'm a Store Operative.	(Shelf packer.)

Sexual inexperience/Virginity
The strict definition of a virgin is someone who has never had
sexual intercourse. Yet, the subject of sex usually includes
lower-key activities such as kissing, petting and masturbation.
You may not have had sexual intercourse, but we would be

very surprised if you have not engaged in at least some potentially preliminary acts. In the loosest sense of the word then, you are not a virgin. If you can re-order this situation in your mind, you'll be able to bluff your way – should you feel any need to do so – with conviction. Bluffing it while naked is much harder, but Chapter 8 may help you overcome any problems. You might prefer (only if genuine) to hide your virginity or inexperience behind family upbringing or religious belief, or simply not to get too involved in sexual discussions. Far better, sometimes, to suggest that you prefer doing things rather than talking about them.

Solo status
Apart perhaps from religious abstinence, you should be careful about divulging long-term, solo status to women. Few really appreciate how much trouble some genuine men can have finding a partner. Most women avoid undue questioning of your past relationships and so you can keep control of what you say and how you say it.

If she asks you if you are solo in front of others, bluff. Her motive is more likely to be disrespect than curiosity. You can always say something quizzical, such as, ''Aha! That's not really for me alone to decide''. If she asks in private or after she has told you she is single, fight your pride and tell her the truth.

Am I prepared to continue along these lines with her indefinitely?

This will depend upon both you and her. Clearly not every relationship can become a marriage partnership. However, a word about selflessness rather than selfishness may not go amiss here. Her biological clock ticks faster than yours and the ideal window for marriage and children is, for her, considerably shorter. Therefore for a man to cling to a relationship out of convenience, or maybe just through lack of thought, long after he knows it cannot be long-term for him, can evolve into a wicked act. That she may seem content is no excuse for ducking your duty to say where you stand.

MENTAL SELF-DEFENCE

Showing women strength of character is a sure way to let them know you live your life by choice, rather than by weakness, driven by guilt.

You need, as the saying goes, to have enough of the devil in you to keep the devil off you. Not only must you be able to parry a little teasing, you must demonstrate that sense of genuine inner strength women so admire.

Many mental self-defence techniques revolve around self-control of your giving. Women are drawn to a man that gives, but one who gives too much (buys all the women in the club a drink), too soon (tells her straightaway that she's beautiful), or to women who don't give back (continues being polite to a woman who has called him a fool) can attract for all the wrong reasons. Most women do not respect unrestrained giving. It is unattractive for the same reasons that self-confidence is attractive; it says a lot about your capacity to deal with life and other people.

Quite a thick skin is sometimes needed when you meet and greet. Regardless of their own (in)ability to take some ill-mannered riposte, certain women will dish out rude or silver-tongued remarks with apparent glee. Some men even take it upon themselves to get in the first cuss but stimulating women by attacking them has never been our way and we hope it's not yours either. There's too much man/woman grief in the world already. The way we deal with female word-feints (more often than not a brash form of flirtation) is simply to counter them with polite repartee.

At a time when culture seems to demand winning at all cost, letting her win can rebound on her to your credit. So don't worry! Actually, if you can also develop a good return of serve, it's one of the most impressive things you can do.

Deflection

Basically this is humorous armour. Deflection is a highly advantageous social skill worth developing. Not only can you block, but you can take all the sting out of an attack. It should always be a first choice defence because nobody gets hurt from it.

Her	*You*
You're not that bright are you?	I know. It's a wonder they let me vote.
Do you call that fashion?	*Expensive* fashion, yes.
Are you a man or a mouse?	Got any cheese?
You look unfit.	No problem. If we date, I'll join a gym.

Other deflection lines for the aggressive woman:

"That's a tight corset you're wearing."

"Are those new shoes?"

"You won't say that when I win the lottery."

(If they give you the silent treatment.) "Shshshsh!"

"Were you in a police cell last night?"

"Do all your boyfriends develop earache?"

Humour – too much – or too little

Many men have such a sweaty paranoia about being unfunny in front of women it blinds them to the fact that women don't relish overdone humour anyway. Steer clear of the belief that a woman will necessarily be yours so long as you make her laugh. This is dangerous thinking and will probably have you acting like a clown in public before you know it. The only clowns that are respected by women are the ones that get paid for their act.

Humour, nonetheless, is a good thing when opening conversations. Wit will help the flow and you should always socialise primed with a few funny stories (there are a few books in the *Right Way* series that can help you here) but a man who can effectively express his passion for a woman is far more desirable than a poor joker annoyingly unable to resist quipping.

Sure, everybody likes to laugh and there is a host of clinical information telling us exactly how beneficial it is, but always remember that a sense of humour is subjective. One's woman's guffaw is another's scowl. So why should you collapse if she doesn't laugh?

If you want your humour to have a wide appeal, concentrate on charm and context. A likeable man is an attractive man but it's hard to be liked if your humour is inappropriate. If she trips over, for example, it's better you help her up and say, "That's why I don't wear my high heels any more" rather than "Had a nice trip?"

Humour without charm can fail its purpose. With it, you can get away with innuendo, corn, banter, pause-covering and conversation mistakes. If she doesn't get your joke, for example, cover any inferiority she may feel by inserting a joke at your expense, i.e. "Sorry! I missed the point of that joke too", or "Next time I'll remember to make it funny".

The pressure on men has lessened slightly through the increasing female assertion in our culture. More and more women are ready to display their ability to inject humour into conversations. The increasing success of female comediennes is both a cause and effect testimony to this. If you meet a funny woman, give her space. Suppress any competitive instincts. Why outdo her? Laugh and she will laugh with you. Throw in a complimentary quip if you wish but let her feel she's the funny one, unless of course she tries to run you down.

Whether or not you are very witty, or consider yourself much funnier than the woman with whom you're talking, please resist any urge to humiliate her publicly. No-one really likes being made fun of. Banter is fine in the right context and most women are robust enough to take the odd ego deflation but never use your rapier wit to embarrass. If you want to risk such fun, at least do it when no-one else is listening.

Opinions and arguments
The essentials of charm should be understood by everyone but you may also need to balance your compliments with some

salty opinions. This way you show her that you are a real person, not just a charm machine. In practice this means not being afraid to disagree with her, or even to argue. Do you seriously think there will be no arguments if you have a long-term relationship? Men are notoriously reluctant to argue because it seemingly lowers the chance of intimacy, but you don't need to have a full-blown row on every topic. Just be prepared to disagree enough to let her know that you have your own mind. Even those women who like to be in control don't want a permanent yes man. More important perhaps than arguing is showing willingness and the ability to state your opinions on a subject. It is best if you react to something she's said rather than pull some view point out of the air. However, you need to be wary of certain delicate subjects which may divulge your insecurities. Be prepared to give her something of your hopes, dreams and views, for example:

"You're lucky you like your job. I want to change mine because . . ."

"I like travelling too, but I'll never visit Timbuctoo again because . . ."

"I know you like them, but I think the Beatles were over-rated . . ."

Arguing
Whatever your opinion, being able to express it well will always earn you kudos. Always try to come from a position of strength, not just because you like the sound of your own voice. You don't have to know the director of a film to argue its merits on the basics of plot, acting and script but you do need to have seen the movie. If you must risk seeming like an ignoramus by debating a topic you don't know much about, just qualify it by saying, "Well, I don't know for sure but I'd guess that . . ."

If she really tries to draw you on some matter about which you know little, don't get flustered, just stall:

"I might have a view but I don't really want to express it now because I'm not in possession of enough verifiable facts"

or

"I'm sorry. I don't follow [subject] because it doesn't interest me sufficiently."

It's one thing knowing all there is to know about cars, football or trains but these subjects don't crop up as often as you might like. So the trick is to broaden your horizons. You need a healthy (data) bank balance. Apart from any subjects you love and know lots about, try to maintain a keen awareness of contemporary and newsworthy affairs and keep a mental note of anything you find especially ridiculous or funny. Such items often play well as conversation points.

To help you develop your opinion skills further, try the following. Read two daily newspapers with contrary editorial policies and compare them. Watch one quality TV debating show a week. Actively join in discussions with people you consider more intelligent than you. This can help expand the depth of your knowledge on differing topics enormously. Remember, she doesn't have to agree with you, even if she's wrong. If she does concede defeat, try to win graciously, "Okay, let's agree to disagree!" And use the same line if she's winning!

Confrontation

This may be a provocative term but confrontation with care sometimes has to be a necessary part of your dating character. While arguing shows that you have your own mind, confrontation shows that you are willing to stand up for yourself. Only testy men who can start arguments with the speaking clock will actually enjoy confrontation and it should be reserved solely for appropriate use. Confrontation is most effective when women give you a leg-up onto the moral high ground. For example, in circumstances such as when she agrees to a date without pressure but cancels without explanation, or reacts in a nasty way to your polite approach, or has turned out to be of the sort who embarrass you during dates but throws a hissy-fit if you aim a jibe back, you need not fall prey to excuses about hormones, bad-hair days or baggage. You are on strong ground for making your feelings clear, politely and firmly. Indeed, if you don't, she may mistakenly regard you as soft rather than tolerant.

Eloquence is not necessary for effective confrontation. The will to confront is. Hopefully any need for confrontation will be in private, but suppose for a moment you are put to the test in public. Firstly, don't worry about the fact that you may not have the verbal ammunition to give replies that will impress all and sundry. Your main objective is to avoid suffering in silence. If others present take note that you deserve in return the respect that you give, all to the good, but don't let that become your main concern. The real trick is finding ways of letting the steam escape without putting her on the psychiatrist's couch or involving the local constabulary. Remember there are laws about slander.

Following these principles will help. You don't need to swear or shout, just be steadfast. Stick to the point of confrontation. Try not to be distracted by her insults and jibes however many people are laughing with her. Be prepared for her to get angry. If she has marked you down as a shy guy, how dare you contradict her assumptions and challenge her?!!! Depart once you've effectively made your point. Refuse to trade insults or continue some circular argument. Be prepared for her not to admit to what she did. Pride cuts both ways.

Never be so pompous as to blame everything on her. Always leave her a way to save face. You are, after all, trying to form relationships, not create enemies.

NEVER, EVER GET PHYSICAL!

Helpful lines to use in confrontation
"Shouting at me isn't going to win the argument/change my mind." "May we have a calm discussion?" "Oh well, that's a whole different argument." "Let's stick to the point, please." "All I want is the same respect that I give you."

As an example of how to confront, let's consider the sensitive matter of what to do after a woman has failed to turn up for a date. You need to deal with it directly, even if it means accepting the possibility of rejection by asking her how she feels. Women may well hate to be put on the spot like this but they should also know that being direct is the best way to deflate anger – perhaps most of all when the truth is that they don't really want to begin a relationship or continue in one at risk of finding themselves out of their depth.

Him: Hi Jenny. Are you okay?

Her: Oh. Hi John! I was just going to call you to apologise. Something came up. Sorry about that.

Him: And you didn't have time to call me?

Her: Hey, don't get heavy; I said sorry.

Him: Well, you've got all my numbers. My time is important Jenny; you should have phoned me.

Her: Okay, okay; I said sorry.

Him: All right, I suppose it must have been necessary. Have you got it sorted out now?

Her: Yes I have.

Him: Shall we rearrange then?

Her: Errr, I tell you what; I'll call you.

Him: Hang on a minute, what are you trying to tell me?

Her: . . .

Him: Jenny, look, I don't know what's going on but I know I like you and want to see you again. Do you want to see me?

Her: (Pause) No.

Him: Okay, not what I hoped you'd say but I can live with that. At least now neither of us need waste more time and, if we see each other among friends or company, it doesn't need to be embarrassing.

A downbeat ending perhaps, but realistic. At least John knows where he stands. He's left the door open and he's let her know that he likes her.

Turnarounds

These are a halfway house between deflections and confrontation. In private they are devastating – hurtful and out of order. In public some are put-downs but they may offer ways with a sporting chance of turning disrespectful statements back in your favour – provided you can carry them off with a big wide grin and the company you are in is disposed, generally, to be on your side.

Her:	*You*
Is that the best you can do?	No! I'm holding back for the right occasion.
I know what you want and you're not having it.	I hadn't thought of *that*!
I don't think you're funny.	That's good. I want us to be serious.
I don't think you know much about women.	Thinking may not be your strong point.
You look desperate.	It takes one . . .
The future is female.	Yes, so my maid tells me.
You're not much of a man, are you?	No! Just man enough not to rise to your nonsense.
You get on my nerves.	Ouch! How many amps was that?
You think you're funny.	Not as funny as you, though.
You think you're the big cheese, don't you?	Yes. There's only room for one.
You're so ugly.	What? Am I a mirror?
You're such a fool.	Coming from you, that's the *good* news.

CAUTION: HANDLE WITH CARE

Resist trying to argue every comment from a woman. Take things in fun when that's how they're meant. Only a hostile or demeaning jibe deserves your retort – polite, firm, quick-witted if repartee is your forte. But even then, sometimes the best reaction is no reaction. If you can carry off a blasé response or face jokey rudeness with like banter, the woman in question may well switch rapidly from being aggressive towards you to giving you considerable respect. You may just break through what was all a front devised to cover up shyness and fear.

Rejection

Should confrontation go beyond bounds, be prepared to walk away. Rejection is your most potent weapon when faced with uncompromising disrespect from a woman, even though it does not need to involve direct confrontation. Rejection removes attention, and that's painful for anyone. This is why it's the best way of dealing with any such games as those she is better equipped to win. Just accommodate her forays until you feel you stand to lose too much, then switch off. This sends out positive messages that you have a measure of control over your desires. You give but you can also take away. Practical examples of rejection are: if she tries to lose you in the club after inviting you to go with her, don't follow, just do your own thing; if she always ignored you when you were single but now wants to know you when you're settled with a partner, why give her your time?; if you're on a date and she starts flirting outrageously or sexually with someone else, tell her you don't like it and if she continues, pay the outstanding tab, tell her you have done so, and leave. Of course, all relationships can be stifled without reasonable give and take and she's entitled to be good friends with others, just as you are but, if she's like that on your intimate dates, what is she going to be like in a relationship?

Caution: handle with care

Rejection is not a game. Before you use it, ask yourself if you can stand never talking to the woman in question again, because that's what might happen. If she does contact you to apologise for her behaviour, resist the urge to lord it over her. She will respect you even more.

Praise

Insults are one thing; not being appreciated is another. Men have to accept that they may never get the praise from women that they may feel they deserve. Believe it or not, some women do still go for the outdated, misguided and immature "treat them mean, keep them keen" philosophy. Upbringing may account for some of this; however, if she gives you her attention and later her affection, that's praise enough.

Incidentally, every one of these Mental Self-Defence techniques here described also works with men. You need not let snide remarks by other men go unchallenged; however, you have to be careful because of the readiness with which some situations, notably confrontation, can escalate into unwarranted violence.

Male sharks

Friends who won't ever tread on your toes or interrupt your promising conversations are worth their weight in Viagra pills. As you probably know though, you can't expect too much from some men when women are on the agenda. Sharks are the "friends" about whom you need to be most on guard. These are men who will consistently risk your friendship by desperate competition for a woman.

Spotting a shark's fin is not difficult. He will try to: butt into your one-to-one conversations with women, take your place in the conversation once you leave temporarily, i.e. to go to the toilet, and not allow you back in, even when the woman shows signs of wanting to resume conversation with you; use oneupmanship when women are around; mess with your mind by asking if he can move in on a woman that you clearly had your eye on first; seduce a woman you still are, or have been until recently, intimate with.

At some time, all friends may display some of the above traits, just as they might innocently harbour indecent thoughts about any love interest you have. The difference is that a shark will display most of the above, most of the time, and try and turn any red-light fantasies he has about your partner into reality.

Just how, though, when their actions are so obvious, do sharks get away with it? They play on male psychology.

Like the original playground bully, sharks bite men who they don't think will snap back. Surprisingly, when sharked, most men fall into this category. The pain may be searing, but ego and pride dictate presenting a calm, collected exterior. You may fear seeming territorial and possessive, especially until you know the woman concerned really quite well. Good reasons for this have been outlined previously but your main weapon is to harpoon sharks immediately, even if it means confronting them in front of women. Remember, the shark's confidence comes from predicting you won't want to endure exposing him publicly. If you surprise him straight off guard, you dent his confidence and also break the hypnotic spell his unbridled risk-taking can have on women. Suppose, for example, a shark asks if he can move in on a woman with whom you've been getting on rather well. You can assuredly afford not to fall into the trap of compliance just to suit him. By what right does he presume to ask such a barbed question anyway? Leave no room for ambiguity in your response. If you feel you have to say "Yes, I really do mind!" before he gets the message, do. Once you've been straight with a shark, he either has to respect your honesty, or show himself up for what you already know he is. A favourite sharking response is then to try and make you feel guilty about your directness on the subject. Here's the way to cut him off:

Shark:	What are you getting upset for? She's not your girl-friend.
You:	That's not the point, what you did was rude and I don't like it.
Shark:	Wow, I never knew you were the jealous type.
You:	Well, now you *do* know.
Shark:	No need to bite my head off, I only asked.
You:	Rough questions deserve rough answers.

If he still tries to bite after you've told him you don't like it, give him the red card. As much as you may enjoy his company for all kinds of reasons, steer completely clear unless or until he promises to change his ways. It's unlikely that he can change but your directness will at least make him respect you, if nothing else. You'll find that sharks don't have many real friends because of their ultra-competitive nature; so if you call time on the friendship, he'll feel it more than you.

DESPAIR

You may shrug off nagging backache but please don't be lax about any deep or prolonged despair. Despair can be a sadistic arsonist who will set your house ablaze, then tie you to your garden gate and make you watch. How do you fight such an enemy you can neither see nor touch, still less, sometimes, describe in any meaningful words? By reminding yourself that you are insured. Time is your insurance and, if used wisely, it can lessen your despair. We have no way of knowing your life story but if it is one of despondency it's a fair bet singledom certainly doesn't seem to help. If your problems are so severe that they even make you apathetic towards [your] approaching women then your priority must be solving them so that you can make progress.

Talk

How are you going to kiss properly if you're always trying to maintain a stiff upper lip?! Forget unofficial "tough-guy" conditioning that dictates men should be self-contained. We are here not contradicting our earlier advice about keeping your insecurities to yourself. Neither do we advocate town-crier displays of your problems. However, it really can help to talk with someone you can trust without question and who would never even consider your "weakness" as ammunition against you. Remember that what you see as "weak" may actually be your greatest strength once your perspectives on life return to normal.

If you have no-one you can trust and are finding it hard to cope, seek counselling. There are strong professional as well as lay networks in most countries. Whatever your specific problems may be, there is probably an interest group that can help you.

As a rule your Doctor should always be the first port of call. A non-existent love-life should not trigger a morose state any more than might a severely battered and let down one – at least not in theory. However, the risk of developing clinical depression, which is a recognisable illness, is a genuine matter for assessment and help from your doctor(s).

Never suffer in silence. Rather than imagine other (foolish) people may think less of you, visit your doctor sooner not later. Be reassured that he or she *can* get you better surprisingly quickly. Substitute courage for any fear you may have of seeking the right help. Your only priority is to get on the mend as quickly as possible.

CAUTION: HANDLE WITH CARE
To get the best out of professional (or lay) counselling, you must be honest with your doctor and those others in whom you may place your trust. But follow your instinct should you smell a rat. Not all experts or qualified medics are good. Some are appalling and you should never put off finding a second opinion if anything worries you.

NEGATIVE DESIRE
There may be a negative personal characteristic or two that you also need to work on. Without seeing you in action, it's

hard to tell whether you have such a ''bone in your body'', but a good starting point is to look at those things which you *like* doing. For example, one of your authors took some while to identify a degree of almost sadistic pleasure he gained out of embarrassing women in public. Needless to say, women avoided being with him, despite his more desirable attributes. Author two preferred to keep his emotions to himself rather too much for his own good. While author three used to talk as if he was the only person in the world who owned a mouth. You need to discover your less lovable qualities and work on them every day.

In our first two chapters we have taken a general approach to intimacy designed to help you achieve a relaxed attitude *before* you meet women. From here on, it's all about meeting women face-to-face.

3

THE HARDEST STEP

At private parties your invitation itself signals belonging within the group coming together. The friendly disposition among all present is conducive to meeting and getting to know new people; the way to a budding romance is generally smoothed for you and her alike. The awful truth about parties, from small dinners to big birthdays and their like, however, is that you must throw some to go to some. No-one likes the scrounger who never returns an invitation. Even your best friends tire eventually.

This chapter, however, is not about private parties, semi-private "charity do's", or whatever. It's about the cutting edge – the tough assignments where you must "learn your trade" – the public venues where you must hone your techniques and where opportunities so often abound.

If you knew the pretty girl in the hotel bar would accept you, then you'd be over like a shot. Whatever reasons you give for delay or non-approach, your main one probably includes some fear of rejection. This fear can wrap around your confidence like quick-drying cement. Only by dealing with it can you take full charge of your relationship destiny. Your chances of meeting "Miss Right" and of seeing her again will rise accordingly. How?

LESSENING THE FEAR
Just knowing more about what *can* be done can make you more confident about approaching.

Bouncing

To modify a famous quote, there are only three certainties in life: death, taxes and rejection by women. Defeatist? No. Realistic? Yes. Most men get turned away from approaches more often than not – no matter what they may tell you! In reality a one in ten success rate is fabulous. At least in the outside world of public venues it would beat our record.

A practical extension of the net-spreading principle of Chapter 1, *bouncing* is the ability to think in terms of *quantity until you meet the quality*. Some girls may not agree. Their desire for attention insists that you persevere with them, or at least don't make them feel cheap by approaching other women in their presence. Sorry, but we no can do! Although you should never set out to hurt a woman, you cannot afford the time to worry about her insecurities when she has seen fit to reject you. There's no harm in setting out for an evening, for example, with the aim of approaching a minimum of three women until you strike lucky.

Not always your fault

Take her rejection on a no-fault basis. From what you have absorbed from our first two chapters, the host of non-personal reasons why she might reject you should help you form a balanced view and move on. Other reasons may suggest that your patience could be rewarded or that there is no chance whatever. See what you think of these:

She's in a relationship

Even though she may have doubts about her relationship, she may prefer the devil she knows rather than you. Many women will not countenance disloyalty; if a relationship is to end, they want this to be clear all round before embarking upon anything new.

Peer pressure

Unless your attraction is magnetic, women, like men, can be unduly influenced by their friends. Without doubt, this is the most annoying factor that may work against you. It is also, unfortunately, one of the most common. Be yourself in their company but avoid giving (potential) wagging tongues anything to wag about.

Compatibility
She may seek compatibility with influences which are most important to her, such as religion, culture, race, age, etc. and mainly outside her control, never mind yours.

Hard to get
Women still resist being viewed as "available". Loss of mystique, rather than pride, is probably at work. Generally, they won't reject outright a likeable approach, but they may not be as instantly responsive as you might wish for. This is only to be expected, so you'll just have to be prepared to maintain your efforts if you think she's worth it.

She's shy
Probably the most underrated reason for rejection. Shy girls are often a forgotten casualty of an unduly feminist culture but this is not a reason to underrate them!

She's not obliged
Just because you plucked up the courage to approach, this doesn't mean she will automatically swoon into your manly arms. She may prefer to chase rather than be chased. She may even resent you because you're so damn confident, just like her bastard of an ex-boyfriend.

Baggage
Talking of ex's, you cannot possibly know how her past experiences have shaped her current relationship agenda. She may just have come out of a painful relationship and be feeling antagonistic towards all men.

Not setting out to hurt you
Not all of us have Teflon interiors (or exteriors). Few women, however, have much idea how much it can cost a man to approach. You may need conscious effort to avoid being over-sensitive because they often simply don't realise they've just stamped your ego into a mushy pulp when they turn you away.

Setting out to hurt you
Having said that, there are some women who will reject you just to see the look of embarrassment on your face. Avoid them. Thankfully, these women are usually easy to spot and, once you are prepared to confront, easy to deal with. It's not often that insecure attackers like these have the talent to defend themselves once you return fire.

The above list is by no means exhaustive, but bearing these factors in mind will stop you taking knock backs so personally.

"He travels fastest who travels alone"
Even if you normally team up with some good mates to go out "on the pull", they might not always be available. We urge you sometimes to give it your best shot *on your own*. One success is enough to prove to you that it's the quickest, most practical way to boost your ego with women. From then on you can cease to rely on the back-up of others, even though they will often be around.

A drink to bolster nerves may not be a bad thing but never rely on alcohol; actually alcohol is a depressant poison and, anyway, slurred speech will scarcely impress. Dress well to give yourself the best chance.

Nothing kick-starts a women's negative assumptions like being approached by a loner, but if you can overcome this (lines to help are given in later chapters), you can overcome anything. The reason for a woman's nervousness about a stranger on his own probably lies in the importance and power of the social fabric that underpins any civilised community of people, be it a country or merely a club. Rogues, cads, perverts and misfits rarely attract a strong circle of good friends and so, until she can be reassured by meeting with some of your real pals, her caution is very understandable.

It follows that one of the most valuable things you can do in life – and which money cannot buy – is to cherish your friends. Build up a network, not only of those upon whom you may rely from time to time, but who can rely upon you equally. She is bound to judge you to some degree when she knows who your friends are, and by whether she feels instinctively that you *belong* in good company; so maintaining your circle should be viewed as a lifelong quest. In any event, real friendships are the very soul of life, so be assured your efforts will never pass, in the longer run, unrewarded.

Can you keep sex off-limits?

You can remove a lot of pressure from yourself if you restrict your immediate ambitions on making an approach to any woman, to simply finding a new friend. Being (genuinely) prepared to make and nurture a platonic relationship frees your mind to get to know her as the individual she is (and vice versa!). Indeed, you are hardly going to acquire the well-rounded social life described above if you cannot exercise this level of self-control over your passionate self.

Acting the brush off

If you can handle rejection without showing distress, this will disappoint any woman setting out to hurt you. And your sense of calm will probably not pass unnoticed by other females, any one of whom could be your next target, who happen to witness such an event.

There are four main ways to mask the pain of rejection: (1) Smile. (2) Relax your jaw. Facial tension is a giveaway that you are cross or angered. Clench your fist instead (but keep it firmly behind your back). (3) Keep eye contact with her whilst she's in full flood. Don't look around at others, no matter how loudly they're laughing at her put-down. (4) Defend yourself with humour; for example, you might declare with a grin, "Dear me! Give me something to break!"

INCREASING YOUR CHANCES OF SUCCESS

Cover
Never be too obvious. For women, desperation is the opposite of attraction. Even a head swivel can betray your hand too early. Snatch any glances you need from a respectful distance. Or perhaps be content for a good friend to do the honours initially for you.

When among your own friends at a promising venue, mask any burning desire to chat up all and sundry, by being seen to enjoy your friends' company and conversation. Keep talking, even if it's just about the weather. As long as your conversation is not overhead, solo women will assume you've got your love-life well under control. This makes you more attractive to whomever you may choose when you do decide to make a move. If only she knew . . .

Knowing when to approach
Women are much more subtle than men about showing an interest in being met. Things are changing, with more and more women discovering the pleasures of being direct, but most still prefer to retain a greater degree of decorum. Therefore you need awareness and alertness so that you pick up even tell-tale signs. Watch for: women in groups who look bored or who keep looking around even while they talk amongst themselves. Perhaps one of them will return your glance for a moment or two longer than would be normal in such a social gathering. Apart from a direct approach, you won't get a stronger signal of female interest than this. If you are attracted to her, do try not to hesitate too long after she gives you this green light. It's surprising how much a woman's self-esteem can be damaged if her interest is not returned. She may well be teasing, she may even be fantasising over

your good looks but, if you don't follow up, you'll never know for sure.

Never *initially* admit that you noticed her looking at you, by the way. You will make her feel self-conscious and instantly raise her defences.

* Watch for women who seem to have eyes for several other men. They may not be looking at you but, if the men they're looking at don't want to approach . . .

* Take note of any who make repeated eye contact with you. This is another strong signal. Don't pay undue attention to one glance or misinterpret the fact that she looks away quickly. She may well not want you to get the wrong idea but this hardly applies if she keeps catching your eye.

* Women with a good sense of composure about them who lack defensive gestures and are clearly relaxed in body and mind may be in a receptive mood too. As may those who don't seem too impressed by nearby men with larger-than-life personalities. (You may find out later that actually they are jealous rather than uninterested, but it's worth your approach anyway.)

Never overlook the women nearest to you, even those who do not conform to any of the previous signs. Their very proximity should make your move easier.

Always look for signs of male company. Men who are with women you desire may be brothers, friends or they might have just introduced themselves that night, but if a woman looks to be enjoying "his" company in any "item" sense then retire gracefully. Women sometimes (naively perhaps) use the opportunity of being with a partner for gazing around at other attractive men without encouraging undue attention. However competitive you may be feeling, don't approach. Treat those guys as you would like to be treated yourself – by not treading on their toes.

CAUTION: HANDLE WITH CARE

Women rarely attend social functions alone. Think before acting hastily. Is she watching the entrance waiting for someone (probably a man)? Has she placed herself in a highly visible area? (People on their own tend not to draw attention to themselves.) Does she keep checking her watch as if wondering whether she's going to be stood up? Does she wait a while before buying a drink? (Other than when waiting for her friend(s) why would she not buy a drink straightaway?) If you still reckon she is on her own after a respectable time has passed, try. Even if not free, she may be grateful for your company, meantime, until her own arrives. When or if that happens be prepared to withdraw discreetly; make a well-mannered exit without being asked. Who knows? You may be invited to join in.

When not to approach
Apart from male company, most of the valid reasons for non-approach are personal rather than circumstantial. It is unwise to approach, for example, when you're ill. There's no point in talking to the girl of your dreams if all you manage to do is sneeze on her. Neither should you approach when you feel especially low or negative and your ego won't take the rejection. Take time out and recuperate as discussed in Chapter 2. Don't be the gambler addicted to the spin of the wheel. Lastly, unless you're the type that responds best to a challenge, don't approach just because your friends are egging you on; make sure you do it because *you* want to. Try to avoid women who are significantly taller than you. Preference for a taller man is perhaps the most universal of all female physical desires. A big adverse height difference is hard to overcome. It's not impossible (is anything?) but it is very difficult. You have been warned!

Always be respectful of a woman who seems defensive, sullen or unresponsive. Let someone who already knows her help to mend her mood. Women who are busy or harassed, i.e. barmaids in busy pubs, women trying to catch trains and women who are actively encouraging the attentions of several men, are best left to get on with what they are doing. Also avoid women who seem extremely upset or worried. However, it can't hurt to ask out of genuine concern whether you can help. If accepted, give your help on that basis. Ask no more at that time. A distressed woman may feel very uncomfortable if you outstay your welcome. She may be happy to cry on a strange shoulder for a short while, but this is definitely not to be construed as any sort of invitation.

GO FOR IT
Women appreciate direct approaches. Avoid half-measures. The more first moves you attempt, the easier they become. These tips have often helped us just prior to making an approach:

Imagine her
When daunted by the immediate prospect of approaching a woman, it's easy for that familiar pedestal to appear. Remove it. Instead, imagine her crying uncontrollably. You'll find this instantly makes her seem less intimidating.

Expect resistance
Polite rejection need not be confused with normal resistance which remains the unofficial dating right of all women – not to make it too easy for men. Responses of the latter sort may seem facetious, cheeky or even arrogant but all provide hooks on which for you to hang further conversation. Go for it!

Outright hostility is uncommon but, especially in the major cities, it seems that the stressful nature of modern life may condition some people into developing defensive, suspicious mentalities. There can be no excuse. Move on straightaway. Such women are best left to their own devices.

Tap into laughter
To relax, remind yourself of a joke or humorous situation that always makes you smile.

Adjust your breathing
Consciously breathe quietly and deeply through your nose for a few moments.

Focus your thoughts
Try and tune out everyone else, even buzz and chatter from friends you are with.

Countdown
Ask a friend to count you down (discreetly) from twenty to zero but tell yourself to go when he reaches five. If you are alone, the friend *can* be you!

Do's and don'ts
Once you've started your move, *do* be polite and speak clearly. If (good) friends are with you, an early invitation to meet them can take some pressure off for you. (Always be ready to play your part when it's your turn!)

    Don't touch her, offer to shake hands (see below) or move in so close that you encroach on her personal space. It isn't always a good idea either to offer to buy her a drink immediately, or to ask her name straightaway (see also below).

Hand shaking
Avoiding a hand shake may seem a strange instruction but many women simply refuse to shake hands unless it's a third-party introduction, a professional meeting or names are being swapped. If none of these applies, a polite "hello" nod will do nicely.

Names
In the pre-dating game, genuine names are not always given freely. Give her a few minutes to get comfortable with you before asking. If she doesn't ask yours in return, this may mean she is not much interested or just that she doesn't want to reveal her hand as yet.

Drink buying
This is a contentious issue but one where practical experience has convinced us that our advice here is often correct. Hasty drink-buying can make a woman wary: "If he thinks he can woo me with lots of drink, he's got another think coming!"; or greedy: a thoroughly materialistic woman may pretend to be interested only to keep you buying! Keep your money in your pocket is our advice, at least until you've established some sort of rapport and can judge for yourself. By then, if you do choose to offer, you won't mind spending the money! We tend to backpedal rapidly from women so blatant as to *ask us* to buy them a drink – unless it's with their money . . .

WOMEN IN GROUPS
In social settings, most women prefer the safety in numbers. Perhaps group interaction also exists to take the functional boredom out of going to the toilet! This means that to talk to one woman whom you fancy usually requires including her *and* her friends within your initial approach.

Not so solid
A little understanding of female groups may help calm your nerves. You need not assume that when they're in groups women are necessarily as solid as sisters, ganged up to thwart you. Far from it – the whole purpose of joining together is normally to help each other go with the flow. You'll very quickly realise you've stumbled upon friendly territory with this kind of group. An opportunity to meet the girl you chose should not slip you by too easily.

Nonetheless feelings of harboured resentment, simmering jealousy and hidden dislike can percolate the atmosphere among women together just like the unfriendly dynamics which may act to one degree or another within any male group. Sometimes the only thing bonding these women will be a desire to go out to the same places, just as you may be out with someone you don't really like for the simple reason that it's better than being alone. You're likely to recognise such tension pretty swiftly. Don't try and split women at war with each other (this is only likely to bring them closer together), still less be fooled into thinking that you have to take them all on! Simply pick out a friendly one and ignore the others.

Miss "Negative"

You need, however, to approach all groups with a flexible attitude because, even amongst a friendly gathering, there is nearly *always one* woman who will be negative about your approach and the loveliest girl can be caught up with the awkward squad sometimes. Either way try to give Miss "Negative" your undivided attention first. Her only motivation may be shyness. "Stoop to conquer" and you may then scoop the pool . . .

If she refuses to defrost, your only option is then to concentrate whole-heartedly on the others – and place your trust in the reality that is female competition. (Miss "Negative", incidentally, is easy to spot, disrupting your approach by demeaning it, instantly mentioning boyfriends, talking across you, whispering in her friend's ear, trying to pull the other friends away, etc.)

Landed amongst a nest of "negative" vipers be ready to endure their scorn long enough to let that gorgeous mermaid swim to the top – as she may well then do . . .

You must hone your skills at defusing negativity. Otherwise, as we have warned before, female loyalty and the peer pressure influence of a Miss "Negative" will too often beat you.

Successful ways to approach women in groups

If you're with friends
Ideally, approach in equal numbers. Send in a front-runner; then back him up as soon as he's delivered his opening line. This is less threatening for the women but remember, the more time one man, no matter how entertaining, is left on his own with two or more women, the more chance there is of a Miss "Negative" emerging.

It's usually pointless to stake claims before you start. Let things settle down as you help each other along. If a mate hits lucky with the woman you preferred – well, you win some, you lose some!

If you're on your own
Approach women in groups of three or more to lessen your risk of being shot down by a Miss "Negative". Hold back from your prime move until the girl you like in the group is alone if you can. You may have a long wait; meanwhile, make friends with her friends!

When some other men approach, jump on their bandwagon! However, only do this if the men are outnumbered by the women, otherwise you may cause more trouble than it's worth.

If you like *all* the women, test the water both collectively *and* individually . . . you should soon make up your mind!

Between two *desirable* women, go first for the less classically beautiful one. Take the brunette rather than the blonde, curvier of the two. Even if your goodwill is not appreciated, you are likely to pique the interest of her friend, who may wonder why an obvious charmer like you didn't choose her first. Then the choice will become yours.

We grant that the above advice is harder to take if, as often happens, the contrast in looks between the two women is great. Then the reverse psychology tends not to work unless the plainer woman has oodles of self-confidence – sufficient to believe you prefer her to her attractive friend. If in doubt, therefore, go for the good looker first.

DEALING WITH BEING APPROACHED
Although still a little unusual, women, especially younger women, can now enjoy the freedom of choice to approach men without raising too many eyebrows. Every man is likely to be approached by a desirable woman at some point in his life. Hold onto this thought when you socialise, so as to be ready.

Forget preconceived notions about women who approach

(unless justified by some subsequent behaviour). She must have good taste. She just approached you! However, hide any surprise you feel. Showing it could make you vulnerable to a tease but, more important, could cause genuine hurt were she then to feel she had behaved in a manner unbecoming to women.

A bona-fide approach is a very strong signal. Show friendly interest, let things develop and she will feel that her choice was the right one. You have no need to prove yourself by trying to take charge of the role reversal.

Components of a genuine approach

A female approach may just be a nudge aside at the bar when there's plenty of space available either side of you; or it may be an unsolicited line of seeming innocence such as:

"I saw you when you came in." Body language may clue you in too.

Questions like: "Do you know where the toilets are?"; "Do you know how to get to . . .?"; "Have you got a light?" are probably *not* approaches.

Open-ended questions may well be: "Where are you from?" (Why does she want to know?); "Are you two brothers?"; "You think you're cool don't you?" (And so does she!) "You're not as loud as your friends, are you?" (Does she go for the quieter type?) "Do you want to have sex with me?" (Some women prefer to be vague!)

Compliments are another favourite pass. Respond gracefully; e.g., if she says "I like your shirt," say "Thanks. I guess we've both got taste". Such replies have been known to turn round an approach from flirtatious to serious, but don't stress yourself trying to create the perfect reply. Straightforward courtesy should further conversation.

Ignore crude pinches, grabs, intentional bumps, etc., which would cause an outcry if perpetrated by you. Dating-game double standards turn us off. However, that's just our opinion and you may feel differently if you like her and the circumstances make her gesture forgivable.

SPECIAL WOMEN
Special women require special approaches.

Customer servers
For receptionists, barmaids, travel hostesses and those with similar duties you've got to remember that it's *their job* to be friendly. You need to decode whether there is some genuine attraction there. Does she serve you with an extra flourish? Does she immediately remember your last order or visit? Does she engage you in conversational subjects outside her work remit? Does she mention within earshot that she stayed in over the weekend? Or does she talk freely of her boyfriend?

If you see her in a place you visit regularly such as a squash club, watch her body language especially carefully when you first suggest you would like to take her out. Great diplomacy here, if she says "No, thank you", will save both of you much later embarrassment. Should you make another move later? Only if her signals turn remarkably in your favour.

Age
Taste and perceptions change. Never fall *completely* for the stereotypes of naive, rogue-loving youngsters or cynical toyboy-hunting seniors. However, the general assumptions that as they get older, women become more selective (which may work in your favour) and more appreciative of kindness (which will definitely work in your favour) hold true, so don't discount her just because she's mature.

Approaching beauty
This little-known secret of attraction is that beautiful women are addicted to the attention that they get from men, even though they often wish they could find the "off" switch. Give them controlled attention then, and you will always have a chance, especially if you're the only man brave enough to approach. And, if you want to up the ante still further, approach the most confident women in the group, the one who acts most independently and who will probably be inclined to

go for you regardless of what the others think.

But . . . you need to be honest with yourself if she and you are far apart on the scale of attractiveness. Can you handle the jealousy and paranoia that may come your way if a relationship starts? If you think you can, or are willing to try, then go for it. What you learn about yourself will make the risk worthwhile, even if the relationship isn't.

Foreign women
She's abroad, away from restrictive influences and all you have to do is respect her person – or so you may think! In practice, any cultural relationship constraints from which she may have escaped are replaced by similar baggage you have in your own country. Remember that a foreign woman will be just as proud of her background as you may be of yours. If you can adjust to all this and spend time with her, regardless of any language difficulty and her foreign status, you will instantly increase her affection for you. Later on, you may each need to accommodate any fundamental differences between your two cultures and upbringing, but you will find that intimacy and love can bridge ''impossible'' gaps.

EASY WOMEN
Crass male assumptions of easy availability linked to such things as profession, country of origin or dress, demean. There is often fire behind smoke but no woman likes to be thought of as easy. No matter what associations come to mind when she tells you where she's from or what she does, keep them to yourself. Otherwise you'll never know how wrong you can be!

If you *are* right, then it's entirely a matter for you to decide if you want to know her more intimately.

LOCATIONS
Single women always seem scarce because – at least in the public arena – they prefer to keep their status quiet. In fact, they are everywhere and all you need is to be prepared to travel far and wide to meet them!

Traditional venues
If asked to choose between pubs, bars, clubs, weddings and
parties, the last two are far the best places to meet the fairer
sex, as mentioned at the start of this chapter. By far the worst
are clubs. Yes, they can be quick-fire but what they don't tell
you in the brochure is that the women tend to be shallower,
more defensive, more intimidating in clubs than anywhere
else. Of course, there are exceptions but control your expectations. The saving grace of clubs is that they are among the best
places to go to if you're on your own. The distraction of the
music and dancing covers any gaffs in your approaches.

CAUTION: HANDLE WITH CARE
Going to a club with a girl you've just met can be a giant
let-down. You can avoid this by carrying a wheelbarrow of
self-control and not drawing even the slightest attention to the
heat of the situation: banish lines like: "Once we get inside
the club, you don't have to stick with me"; or "I'll go with
you, but don't worry, I won't try anything" (for all you know,
she may want you to try something).

Late night bars
These are usually more brightly lit than clubs and cheaper, and
you can normally hear yourself talk. These plus points make
bars our favourite late-night locations. However, fewer
patrons inevitably means less choice. Don't let this worry you
unduly, though.

The downside of busier environments is that there is almost
too much choice. While this may cater for your need for
variety it also warps a woman's sense of selection, making
them even more fussy than usual. Whereas, in less busy places
(although it may be true that it is harder to brush off rejection),
women are generally more accepting.

Favourite venues
You need at least four or five rendezvous where women also
congregate, to avoid familiarity breeding disinterest among

any female "regulars". Week nights often sport a quite
different clientele so do vary your haunts!

Unconventional places

State-of-the-art alertness and a little applied "luck" can
engage you in conversation with a woman when you (or she)
least expect it. After that, who knows? From lift journeys to
traffic jams, being prepared to risk opening your mouth is all
that counts – along with good manners. Wait for some hint of
interest (unless time is of the essence) before you make an
approach. Even if she does encourage you, she'll still be
cautious. Remember, to her mind, you may be intriguing, or
even amusing, but until she knows you better, you're just
another potential nut-case! If you meet blank rejection, retreat
immediately; play it cool. Even say "Sorry I've interrupted
your thoughts". Her dignity intact, she may decide to respond
after all.

Dating agencies

Introductory agencies may play a very useful role if you work
long hours, are new to your area, travel a lot or, for whatever
reason, need a starting point. Concerns about compatibility or
having to spend money upfront are minor compared to the
benefits. You meet nice women often in a comparable position
to your own. Provided you're willing to be discreet [about
how/where you met] should your date prefer this, it's a good
way to widen your circle of friends. It's also a wonderful way
to sharpen up your dating skills – to discover first-hand what
women like and how to relax and enjoy life in their company.

   We suggest you check any agency out carefully beforehand.
Does it, for example, belong to an industry association whose
members agree to abide by a set of guidelines and through
which unsatisfied customers can have access to complaints
procedures? Even this is no cast-iron guarantee; few creden-
tials are where money is involved! Your best recommendation
is from friends. Second best may be from your first meetings
through the agency.

Consider: how personal is the service the agency promises? How relevant are questions you are asked? Will you be dealing with the same person when setting up dates? How will he or she portray you? How accurately do you feel prospective dates are being described to you?

Compare agencies on cost, confidentiality and also on how sustainable the promises they make appear to you. Just how likely is it, for example, that some huge number of dates can all be ideally suited to you?

Personal ads
To increase your chances of compatibility reply only to adverts in media that are on your wavelength; however, any advert that speaks directly to you is worth a reply. Imposters from the oldest profession should be obvious enough to miss. If you place your own ad, just three principles really matter: be positive, be brief, be honest.

Responses
The telephone has largely superseded the written word here but do write if you prefer or this has been requested. If you phone, be ready for the ubiquitous answerphone! Take time out to prepare what you're going to say. Gear your reply to her ad. Speak clearly, calmly, confidently. Always leave **your** name and contact number.

When you speak directly keep it natural and polite. If you write, do so legibly, to the point and on nice stationery. If writing is not your strong point seek the help of a good friend.

Ad abbreviations
No TW's: No time wasters. GSOH: Great sense of humour. WLTM: Would like to meet. WLTMS: Would like to meet similar. NA: Non-attached. NS: Non-smoker. ACA: All calls answered. ALA: All letters answered. LTR: Long term relationship. OHAC: Own home and car.

Good manners
It is rude not to answer every letter, or bother replying to call messages – even though this may test your stamina if your ad mentions your seven-figure bank account! You needn't necessarily scribe some personal response to each written reply; a suitable note in photocopy, with space to hand write her name, is acceptable if you are not wanting to take things further. Always send back photographs. On your answerphone you could cover yourself using a timespan clause as: "If I don't return your call within a week then I'm sorry to say I won't be contacting you".

However, this is pretty impersonal. Nothing really beats your voice coming on the line. You arrogant bum!

Sports clubs, political parties, theatre followers, bellringers, you name it

Chase your current hobbies and interests or try something completely new. You'll soon meet like-minded, friendly people but be careful. Don't join these groups expecting them to be the answer to your partnership dreams. Approach them for what they are, widening your interests, your contacts, your person. If you meet your match or perhaps your matchmaker, treat this as a lovely bonus.

Personal development courses

Dance classes are a favourite of both sexes. After a while you should find you can enjoy the intimacy of a nightclub atmosphere without the pressure. Take your time. Forget dating possibilities; dance with all and sundry. Becoming a good dancer commands great respect which should stay with you all your life, ready for more intimate dancing whenever such opportunities happen along.

The personal development heading covers a huge range, from meditation to powering up your business skills. Many such groups involve teamwork and role-playing, both of which can turn weaknesses you may have on the socialising front into your greatest strengths. Go for these. Women do too. Or become a charity volunteer helper where you will meet lots of people. There are single women everywhere if you look in the right places and, provided you are genuinely interested in their subject, you will have an instant connection with them.

Shared accommodation

Tread carefully! When you move into a new place or a desirable woman moves into yours, you won't win any respect by going too fast. You'll get to know her soon enough, whether or not other guys (including any also sharing the property) may appear to be ahead in the running. Make sure she really is the girl for you and watch for signs the feeling is mutual before making any move. This way you won't make a complete prat of yourself.

Internet

Opportunities for the computer literate abound but the jargon and net-expertise are beyond the scope of this book. Suffice to say that good manners and common sense apply as they do throughout our text and that a blind date remains a blind date however you make your first connection.

4

GETTING IN

Now it's time to start talking.

Take your pick from the arsenal of openings we provide. The lines are presented in ways we feel are most workable, but that doesn't mean our text is sacred. Once you understand the principles you can adapt or adjust them, or go impromptu. For real winners match what you say to the time or place or link in to any current topic of conversation.

CHAT-UP LINES

To chat or not to chat? That is the hesitation. Ignore the derision which chat-up lines occasionally attract. You can laugh that off, and practice makes perfect. Women do prefer meetings to arise naturally, but they have the option of waiting. What's your alternative? All conversations have to start somewhere.

Simply saying "Hi" in a friendly manner can be as effective a form of chat-up as any comic opening. Don't give yourself a migraine trying to create some classic swoon-inducing line. They don't exist. Concentrate on lines and delivery which initiate conversation. Make what you say *brief, respectful, question-ended* (when possible) and *lightly witty* when you can. Complex lines may put her back up. Hilarious starters rarely come down without a bump. All you want is a verbal foot in the door, after all. Speak clearly with *charm* not smarm.

Propping up appearances

Except for upfront locations like nightclubs, avoid sounding-off about a woman's biological attributes. Discreet compliments such as "You've got lovely eyes" are well worth using once conversation has developed, but need tact and caution; instant flattery will put off all but the most naive. Disrespectful jokes such as "That's a lovely pair of melons" are right out of order. Women take their appearance seriously. So should you.

Clothes, on the other hand, offer convenient openings. Comments on unisex tops, such as shirts, are less likely to sound effeminate or inappropriate. For example: "That's a nice top" or "I like that top". You might add a cheeky twist: "That's a nice top. (Pause and smile.) Can I try it on?"

Women – not always intentionally – often wear clothes which seem to cry out for a body-oriented comment. Try to resist, for example, if a woman is wearing a crop top or boob tube, a dud like: "Nice you're not wearing much; it won't take so long to undress you". Just say: "Not many women can make a plain top look so chic!" or, for more reaction "Do you think I've got the body for a top like that?"

Trousers likewise can make a neat conversation piece: "Those trousers look good on you. May I have a word with your tailor?"; "Those jeans look better on you than in the advert!"; "I think it's the way you wear those trousers [I like]".

If she has combined high-waist trousers so her navel is obscured with a revealing top, you might risk: "Excuse me, but do you have a belly button?" Spoken confidently with a wink of charm, and bearing in mind that a woman who dresses evocatively usually has the front to handle predictable comments, this line is likely to produce a worthwhile reaction. And that's all you ever need to begin conversation.

A superb tan or beautiful hair, or any other of her physical features upon which a woman has clearly devoted special effort are all acceptable matters to remark upon: for example, "Nice tan. Where have you been?"

For more reaction, try: "Lovely tan, is it all over? Even

between the toes?'' If you're on a foreign holiday in a heatwave, try this – in a deadpan manner: "Nice tan. Been abroad?''

Lastly, on the subject of appearance, never be afraid to try the confident and eloquent, if risqué: "You look lovely!'' Actually, it's more risky than risqué, but it is likely to endear you without putting her on the defensive – provided you *do* say it as if you mean it. (No problem when you do but it's better not to risk sounding insincere if looks are not her best suit.)

Clubs and pubs

In the heady atmosphere of nightclubs, some city-centre bars and trendy theme pubs you can get away with being more direct and extrovert. None of the following is truly disrespect-ful, but they may not play so cool in more sober locations. The more outrageous you make your charm offensive, the more you will need a cheeky, quizzical look to carry it off. Think these through: "I've lost my phone number. Can I have yours?''; "If I were a dentist I'd love to know what your teeth are doing later because I want to take them out''; "Excuse me, I'm doing a charity danceathon. Would you like to contrib-ute?''; "I never thought I'd meet a girl as good-looking as me. Well – not until now!''; "I'm doing a survey on why attrac-tive women don't like chat-up lines. Can I ask you to com-ment?''; "Has anyone ever told you ... (pause for effect) off''; "Excuse me, but we're so close I might knock into you when I've had a few more drinks so I just thought I'd apologise now ...''; "Your bottom is a perfect peach ... (pause) *unlike* my banana!''

If a woman is looking at you or standing very near, try beckoning her over. Then signal sh-sh-sh, lean as close as she'll allow towards her ear and pause just long enough to arouse her curiosity before whispering "Hello!'' Warning: women either love or hate this so it's not a ploy for the faint-hearted.

Corny lines

Turn the risible nature of corn to your advantage. Why strain to be different or risk annoyance by being clever, when you can make such good use of an old line? Tongue firmly in your cheek, corny lines taste great and show that you don't take yourself *too* seriously. Even the oldest sick-bag line of all: "Do you come here often?" works if used correctly.

For even greater effect, deliver your corn as a punch-line after an expectant build-up: "Excuse me" (smile) "this is not a chat up line" (smile again as women normally smile or react at this point with an "Oh yeah?" look) "I just want to ask you a question" (pause) "Do you come here often?"

This method will almost guarantee you some form of workable reaction: "That's terrible"; "I've heard it before"; "I can't believe you said that". To which you can knowingly reply: "Exactly but at least it got us talking . . ."; "I couldn't agree less" (pause) "err, sorry! MORE. Anyway, now we're friends . . ."; "I know it's a shocking line, but I bet my friends I'd use it. Would you mind just laughing to make it look as if it worked . . ."

Old hat it may be but the above line is extremely adaptable. For example, just change one word – "Do you *swim* here often?" – to accommodate an approach in a pool or on a beach.

The same build-up format works with other hackneyed lines such as these: "Are you two sisters?"; "Have you got the time?"; "Haven't I seen you somewhere before?"

Feel yourself getting the taste for corn? Here's some more: "I've been searching for the meaning of life. Now my search is over"; "Hi, I'm new in town. Can you direct me to your heart?"; "If you were a flower. I'd like to be your bumble bee."

If sowing a bit of corn fails, don't blame yourself too harshly. She may just not share your sense of humour. Otherwise you may need to polish up your act but, remember, apportioning blame is a worthless activity, more likely to burn out your confidence than achieve any good.

Trying to be corny about her appearance, by the way, is most likely only to appear insincere. Leave out remarks like: "Is your hair natural?"; or "Your eyes remind me of blue lakes".

Social occasions

The formality of the wedding, the sports club dinner, or whatever may work to your advantage. Conversation tends to arise naturally, using observations you can make about your surroundings. To this end, we've provided brief lists of likely subject props found in different settings as well as some directly topical ice-breakers.

Props for a wedding, for example, might include: the happy couple, the catering, the best man's speech, the romance of the occasion, the characters of the in-laws. To break the ice, how about: "I know officially there's no such thing, but you must be the best lady"; "Will you be jumping for the bouquet?"; "Are you on the bride's or the groom's side?"; "Do you always cry at weddings too?"

Topics from which to draw at a more formal party can be: the host/ess, the music, the DJ, the reason for the party, bad dancers, good dancers, the drinks, the decor, the food, etc. Failing these you can fall back on: "How are you enjoying the party?"; "Are you a friend of . . .?"; "This party reminds me of . . .".

We have found that evening classes and similar activities can be very sociable occasions too, *provided* you're careful not to intrude upon or hold up the learning matters in hand. You could start with a comment about the setting in which the class is held, the difficulty of finding your way there, your motivation for attendance and so on. Then move on to: "What made you take up this form of yoga/this style of painting etc.?"

Unconventional settings can be made social if you are just a little gifted. But be ready to be squashed flat if your line is cornier than a farmer's bunion!

"Washing" lines in your laundrette might flow: "Will I be able to iron my £50 note?"; "I shouldn't wash my dirty clothes in public"; "I'm just a basket case" (as you pick up your laundry basket); or just be straightforward: "Do you have any change for the dryer?". Props in the laundrette are easy: hot (or freezing) atmosphere, waiting time, washing powder, spin dryer etc.

Waiting your turn at your dentist may prove fruitful if you can spin a question or a point of view around the magazines, the reception routine, the flowers, the tension of waiting or whatever. Or try your luck with: "I like this dentist. At least, he hasn't made me scream yet...."; "What's he doing in there? Mining for old gold?" But be sensitive. Stay your enthusiasm if you reckon she is trying to keep the lid on a severe toothache.

In the same way, hold your fire in other medical waiting rooms rather than blurt out any tactless remark. Especially avoid asking what is wrong or invading privacy in any way. It may be a different matter if she ventures to confide in you.

In the park, props abound. Take your pick from weather, birds, ponds, dogs, flowers, trees, roller skates, football players, cyclists, etc. If a woman is feeding some ducks, you could suggest: "They're so greedy; they never throw any bread back". If she is sitting on a park bench, you could tease (with a smile): "Didn't you see the sign saying wet paint?" If she is reading, wait for her to turn the page and try, "Excuse me, is that book as good as the film?" But make sure you have seen the film and can remember some of the story or you may be stuck for words when she replies.

Public transport offers many opportunities for waiting around and sharing moans and groans. The trick is to steer away from these towards things that interest her if you can, so giving her a chance to open up and be forthcoming.

After a delay you could enquire: "Will you miss your connection if this bus doesn't arrive soon?" or "Excuse me, but this crossword clue has got me beaten. Can I read it to you?" or "What time does this ferry dock the other side?"

Any of these can be worked around into further conversation from which you may pick up clues about her interests – upon which to build. You may notice her carrying or wearing sports equipment or some other item which yields an inside track to what she is involved with or likes doing – in which case a suitable opening line should suggest itself.

If you see a woman struggling with heavy baggage, a little old-fashioned chivalry is rarely refused. Just offer: "May I help you carry that?" Any discourteous response cannot hurt you – even if it speaks volumes about her.

REACTION LINES

These are super-effective, not least because they appear to arise naturally with no hint of pre-planning. If you think quickly on your feet you will soon be a "hit"; just stay on watch for comic circumstances you can put to positive use. Unfortunately, not all men have the required "ad-lib" connection between brain and mouth. Not to worry. Even mundane socialising throws up lots of funny situations where "impromptu" reactions can have been rehearsed. The key thing is to react as things happen – to strike while the iron is hot.

For example, poke fun at someone getting tipsy by saying: "That booze is even reaching the parts her boyfriend can't!" or, in a self-deprecating manner: "*I'll* have what he's having!"

CAUTION: HANDLE WITH CARE

You can always poke fun but never poke malice or hurt another person's feelings. Nasty bones are not for keeping in your body.

When you stumble (by accident *or by design*) follow with: "Where's my stunt double when I need him?" When she trips, help her regain balance and say: "You carried that off so well".

In a long burger queue, you might raise a smile with, "What are they doing, growing the onions?"; or "Is this a fast queue or a slow conga?'' Waiting to go into a cinema with a mate you could prime him to say: ''I should have brought my sleeping bag'' which sets you up for the corny answer, ''Don't be silly! Why wake her up?''

If a woman spills drink on you without being aware of it, say: ''That does it! I'm always being taken to the cleaners!'' If she spills a drink while pouring it for you, take the blame at once: ''Entirely my fault – I should have specified 'in the glass' ''.

When she treads on your foot by mistake, swallow manfully but be sure to soothe *her* concern by pointing to your other foot and declaring: ''Everything is all right. I've got another one here.''

If a woman bumps into you during a crowded social occasion, make it your excuse to jest: ''So this aftershave *does* work!''; or ''I'm so sorry. I shouldn't have been standing still''. If you are packed in a public venue like sardines, you can pretend innocence by announcing how much you like a squash so that you can make friends easily. If a group of women near you decide then to laugh at your expense, you can parry with, ''Please share the joke. I could do with a laugh''.

You can react purposefully to any ''fashion statement'' standing out among a crowd: ''Do you think what he's wearing would suit me?''; ''Would my hair do *that*?''; ''Is that cool?''

Whenever you hear a winning bit of banter or repartee, or witness some spontaneous situation that creases you up, make a mental note for re-use another time. Keep a notebook if that helps. The more you work on these, the easier it becomes to spill out a classic line at just the right moment.

CAUTION: HANDLE WITH CARE

Eavesdropping will not earn you brownie points in any company, never mind good company. Even if you cannot help overhearing a woman speaking to others, never let on that you have done so. Only if she returns to the subject once talking with you does it become an OK subject.

BACK-UP LINES

Put-downs are more often feared than received. However, women who would not dream of using one at a private gathering do seem more tempted to do so at public venues, perhaps mainly to show off to their peers, perhaps fearing direct attention (even though that's what they came for!).

Enter that special form of turnaround, the back-up line.

Rest assured that genial approaches, by men who are physically presentable and confidently at ease, are *unlikely* to provoke instant verbal animosity. Resistance though, we must say again, is always to be expected, no matter how smooth you are. Pleasant perseverance can overcome this very natural state of affairs. Often, use of just the right back-up line will reverse in a blink what looked like the instant cold shoulder. Even when you don't manage to gain her confidence, speaking up for yourself appropriately will mostly enable you to leave an approach with your dignity intact.

In the micro-seconds following your opening and her response, you must try correctly to interpret her words, eyes and body language all at once. Depending upon the vibes you feel coming across, this is not so difficult provided you always remember that the main function of your back-up line will be *to further* conversation. Hold on to that purpose and it will deliver the right words to your lips – preferably in the form of a question that invites another reply.

Should you be rebuffed tactfully, take it on the chin, man that you are. However, if instead you get some wholly unwarranted, aggressive verbal flak, you need not feel embarrassed about delivering a "final", witty riposte and walking away. Why waste time? Let her learn her lessons at other people's expense, if she must, but not at yours.

The following back-ups assume negative sounding responses to your openings (positive ones should cause you little difficulty!); however, most of them can be used with a smile *or* a scowl, depending on your estimation of her true availability for a relationship. The lines marked (W) are "walk away" lines that should only really be used in the face of uncalled for and unacceptable nastiness.

Back-up lines to common replies

You're a bullshitter.	How did you know my real name?
	You mustn't judge me by other men you meet.
	Yes, but let's talk about you . . .
That's so corny.	You mean you don't like corn? Think what you're missing!
	Did you say "That's so horny"?
What a *stupid* question!	I guessed you might not know the answer.
	Yes. It was stupid me wasting it on you. (W)
That's a pathetic line.	Never mind! It's got us talking.
	So are the ones around your eyes but I won't shout about them. (W)
That's rubbish.	Give me *some* credit; at least I didn't ask you if you come here often . . .
	Then it belongs in the same bin as your dress. (W)
What's it to you?	With your attitude, not a lot. (W)
No.	That was short and sweet, just like my socks! Anyway, now that we're friends . . .
	That was straight to the point. Do you play darts?
Go away!	To your house? You don't waste time do you?
	With your attitude, it's a pleasure. (W)
I don't want to talk to you.	Okay, why don't you sing/mime?
	It's your loss. (W)

I've heard that one before.	So, you know the answer?
If my man was here . . .	. . . we'd have a threesome!
Do I know you?	Probably, I'm quite famous.
	Sorry, my mistake, you look like a guy I know. (W)

Of course, she may have a further slick answer for almost anything you say, but by then you're in a conversation. The back-up has done its job or you already know she's not your type.

Back-ups when your opening line is greeted by a stony silence
Silence need not crush your spirits, although it may prove a tougher assignment than some of the tricky answers above. The giveaway to her true interest in you will be whether she holds eye contact. Faced by a silent group, target the one who most catches your eye or seems the least shy. Try these: "I don't read minds but I could read a palm or two" (make sure you've read up some basics in palmistry); "What is this, a staring competition?"; "Ladies, I'm not a mind reader; a word or two would help"; "How long is your sponsored silence set to run?"; "Oh no" (feign disappointment) "just my luck to pick an attractive mime artiste to talk to!"

After any of these she may answer or make a rude gesture(!) but, if she's well-dressed or good-looking, you can be ready with: "I was only joking, but I guess our sense of humour is different. At least we have both got our good looks to talk about." Insert "style" for "good looks" if you feel uncomfortable using the former.

She may be foreign, in which case you can bluster: "Our English humour never seems to travel well."

She may be with an English "Miss Negative" friend, who sneers: "I'm English and I didn't find that funny", in which case you've got it made: "Oh, I forgot. You have to have a sense of humour as well!"

If unbecoming silence radiates from a woman significantly

taller than you (we did warn you!) ask: "Do you feel threatened by my height?"

Sometimes you may just have to accept a silent rejection, for example, if a woman successfully avoids any eye contact or simply turns her back, or if women together pointedly talk amongst themselves. Move on to better pastures. Whatever you do, don't react to silence by asking, "Are you deaf?" (rather aggressive if you think about it) or "Why won't you talk to me?" (pleading).

The dismissive wave
All too common a reaction from very arrogant women is to attempt to wave you away. You can cut them off short: "The queen only waves like that from her carriage!"; "Would you like to clean my windows?"; "What sort of aerobics are you into?"

Excuse me I –
Sometimes a woman won't even pause while you get your chat-up line out – before answering back. This shouldn't make you reel onto your back foot. At least she's not afraid to talk!

You: Hi I –
Her: Is this a chat-up line?
You: No. Of course it's not.
Her: Why not?
You: Because they're cheap and tacky. (Pause and smile.) By the way, do you come here often?

You: Okay, I know you're good looking but let's chat. I want to hear whether you're brainy as well.
Her: I hope your brain works better than your looks.
You: I'm a genius, how about you?

You: Good even . . .
Her: Blah! Blah!
You: Are you on voicemail?

Her: Yes, at work.
You: Why don't you switch it off here then?

You: Hello I . . .
Her: We're gay.
You: Really? Then we've all got something in common.
Her: Oh yeah, you're not . . .
You: No. I meant that I like women too!

5

STAYING IN

Wow! She's actually laughed at your inane opening! Now what?! *Now* you have to show you can do more than shoot from the quip.

LISTENING
Always be prepared to listen to, more than you talk back with, a woman you like. Constant interruptions and monologues irritate anybody, male or female. A woman you've known for ages may be prepared to go along with a big-hearted conversation split of 60:40 (guess which side you're on) but a newcomer may well want (and expect) 90:10. We jest not.

Once she's in full flow, cast aside, at least for the moment, the funny stories, the flow-stopping quips from your portfolio; just listen. *Really* listen. This way you will appeal to her desire for commitment – something you can satisfy fully and without further effort, always provided you stop yourself being distracted.

If you do have to interrupt her, break it gently: "I would love to talk to you for much longer but I have to go now"; "I'm 'bursting' . . . but hold that thought and I'll be back in a mo' ''.

QUESTIONING
Before you can listen, she must speak! You need to get her talking with some skilful questions which won't feel to her

like interrogation. Even a shy woman will open up to you, once you become good at this subtle art of drawing her out. Avoid questions which reach a full stop with a one word answer. As a general guide, go for questions that start with any of Rudyard Kipling's "six honest serving men": *where, who, what, when, why* and *how*; and limit questions that start with: *do, if, should, would* – particularly in first encounters as these four easily attract conversation-stopping answers.

We presume no reader would be so naff as to make work the subject of an opening question. However, later on, perhaps after divulging (briefly, mind!) your job or situation, you can usefully raise this topic: "What do you do?"; "How/why/when did you go into that?"; "Where would you like to be by next year?"

Your questions mustn't smack of being too planned. Vary them and relate them to her answers on the spur of each moment. The above general plot might play out like this:

You: What do you do?

Her: (shrugs) I work in the back office of a bank.

You: Something tells me you don't like it?

Her: Not really; how can I enjoy working in a bank when none of the cheques and balances are mine?

You: Nice one! Still, if you don't like accounting, why do it?

Her: The money (sighs), what else?

You: Well, that's half the battle, I guess. I hear the Queen hates her job too, but the money keeps her going! If you could get any job that paid you the same or better money, what would you want to do?

Her: Go on holiday! No, seriously though, there are so many other things I'd enjoy getting to grips with.

You: (Now you're in there) Go on . . .

Notice how a little light, relevant humour, if you can manage it, should keep her responses sparkling along too. Here are some rapid-response lines to help prevent her feeling you are conducting some job interview when she doesn't want the job . . .

Her: You ask a lot of questions, don't you?
You: (Smile) Do you think so?

Then continue, "It's a habit I've borrowed from personnel recruitment. By the way, you've got the job!"; or "How else am I going to find out your credit card number?"; or even "You intrigue me. How else am I to know whether you really are as good as you look?!"

HOT TOPICS
Your best starting handle will often be some observation about her. An accent, a slice of personal history, a strong view – all these can be used to open up a conversation. With a little subtlety you can end up talking about almost anything, but some topics are definitely safer to introduce than others.

If you stray into sensitive areas, show your respect by saying: "Do please stop me if I get too personal . . ." If you're getting on well, she probably won't stop you. However, if she does, *don't you* take it personally; just change subjects. Show care for her and she may care for you . . .

Safe subjects

Careers – Ambitions – Education
You will hold her interest if you can make encouraging noises about her career objectives and plans, but avoid offering dogmatic views (at least for now) about what is essentially her business.

If she is sensitive about, for example, being unemployed or on a low-income, or being a single mother, pay attention; you may be best to leave the subject as soon as you can.

Once you open the subject of ambitions it can go in any direction – not just over the moon . . . Let it meander where it will.

Education usually manages to slip in by the back door when chatting about careers or ambitions. Whether or not a woman is better qualified than you, give praise where it's due. Superior educational experience is not, however, a reason for either of you suddenly to idolise the other. Neither is lack of it any excuse to lower your opinion. To believe otherwise, when life experiences and personality count for so much, is to be immature. Attaching too much credence to education will only undermine your confidence or make you appear too clever by half.

Background
There should be no shortage of material here: ''Is [name of town] home for you?''; ''Do you go home much or see your parents?''; ''How did you like the place you were brought up in?''; ''Would I like it?''; ''How long have you lived here?''; ''Where else have you lived?''; ''Do you have brothers and sisters? What do they do?''; and so on.

Travel and holidays
Another wonderful topic to begin from an open-ended question: ''Do you prefer an active holiday or sunning yourself on a beach?''; ''Does your work take you abroad?''; ''Is it as brilliant there as everyone says?''

Her perspective of others
''Did you read about so and so in the paper?''; ''Did you see that interview they gave on (show)?''; ''Do you know you look a bit like (name someone famous and good looking!); ''Is there someone you'd love to be like?'' all work well. Local gossip, however (i.e. about people she may also know), risks putting your foot right in it and seeming effeminately bitchy. Steer clear!

Leisure-time activities
That's hobbies in old money. Best to use ''everyone has a hidden talent; what's yours?''

Popular culture
Linking into leisure, music or film is usually productive; and it is
by far the safest area for conversation. Strangely, great books are
less so – unless you have already discovered that she loves
reading.

Unsafe topics
Women who know you may excuse opinionated gaffs out of
[misplaced?] affection. A woman whom you have just met need
have no such loyalty. That's why you need to be wary of topics
on which views are likely to be deeply-felt. Religion, politics,
race, drug issues, crime and punishment, and war all spring to
mind as subjects upon which insensitive views can make backs
bristle. Why expose yourself unless *she* brings one up and her
ideas very much coincide with your own anyway? There will be
plenty of safer opportunities to show your independent mind
privately, later, each at the right time and place.

Sport
Be advised that a fanatical fixation on any one sport might,
just might, conflict with a girl's needs for total commitment.
Keep it under your hat for the time being!

Sexual politics
A wrong-footing subject if ever there was one, your best bet is
not to take it seriously; indeed, poke a little fun at it if you
like. Ardent feminists may object, but do they truly seek equal
romance with men anyway?

"You're right, women are better than men at everything.
Cooking, cleaning, ironing, sowing, dusting . . ."; "I wouldn't
mind you earning more than I do, but could *you* handle it?";
"I think it'd be a good idea if women ruled the world – then
they could get paid for moaning!"

Make sure your mental flak jacket can handle the – ahem –
stimulation these lines will arouse!

COVER THE PAUSES

Women can shrug off silences as if they are entirely your fault. They look past you or all around them, start examining the furnishings; not to mention a whole range of aloof gestures seemingly designed to make you feel as wanted as a day-old takeaway. Don't panic. Very often her silence is just an undesirable side-effect of a personal need to disguise her own anxieties. If a woman *really* doesn't want to talk to you, she will normally move away to another group or comment that she's had enough in some obvious way.

So you need not immediately equate pauses with disinterest, still less make an issue of it or apportion blame to her. It makes perfect sense – even for substantial silence – just to look cheery while you think up a new topic. She may come up with one herself – in which case yours, when it strikes you, will be good to hold in reserve.

You might break a pause with a stalling tactic like involving her in your thought process: "Sorry! The old brain's stuck in neutral! What was it I was going to say?"; or perhaps "Are you thinking what I'm thinking?"

Sometimes you can bridge a prolonged gap by linking backwards with humour: "You know when you said you were going to sell your flat? I'm going to sell mine too. Mind you, my landlord will be upset when he finds out"; or " I bet your office isn't as cramped as mine. I share it with a mop and bucket and some guy called Janitor . . ."

Another good ploy, if you are a reasonable raconteur, is to relate some funny episode: "So there we were, stuck in this huge lift, when a dark voice from the back inquired, 'You're probably wondering why I've called this meeting . . .' "; or tell a joke that you know appeals to women (but don't try this unless well-rehearsed and with the punch line already recalled in your mind).

KNOW WHO YOU'RE TALKING TO

In the character sketches that follow we omit those most accommodating of ladies, the relaxed, friendly, women, those

gifted by being able to put *you* at ease. It's the trickier ones –
not necessarily deliberately so – with whom we are concerned.

Nice girls

They may seem a little backward in coming forward or just
appear to be too much in tow with their more vocal friends;
however, they are invariably polite and have rarely even so
much as thought of using a put-down line or gesture. Their
vulnerability makes them a favourite target for bad boys but,
(unfortunately) the truth is, you won't attract a nice girl by
being soft. Men who are nice but firm when they need to
be, however, are just what the compatibility doctor ordered.

So how do you show her from the word go that this is you?
You may need to remind yourself of the principle of equal
weight we discussed in Chapter 1. You may need to be ready
to fend off those who would try to disrupt your conversation
(like a "Miss Negative" in our Chapter 3 or a shark from
Chapter 2). Mainly, however, because she will not be in any
rush to reciprocate the attraction you are signalling by your
approach, you will need to risk being pretty direct:

You: Would you like another drink?

Her: I'm OK with this one, thanks.

You: We don't have to walk up the aisle just because I buy
        you a drink. Why not have a top-up or maybe just
        some more ice to keep it cool between us?

Her: Oh, okay then . . .

You: Would you like to dance (or perhaps with a cheeky
        grin "Would you like to make it with the feet?")

Her: I'm really not a good dancer . . .

You: Thank you for sharing that because neither am I. But
        let's have a go, and whenever either of us wants to
        stop, we will.

Her: No. I'd really rather not.

You: Okay, I enjoyed asking you anyway.

(She said no; time to back off unless she herself extends the conversation.)

Choosy independent

Usually good-looking, young, and open that she likes being single. This can prove to be a red light signal but by no means always so. If she's both pretty and friendly, how come she hasn't been snapped up?

Either she is very fussy, joking or (and this *is* sometimes real) she doesn't actually need a man. Equally, she may just never have met the man who can fire her neurons.

You will need good judgment here, because other alternatives are that she has been badly hurt and is simply scared of risking that happening ever again, or that she has swallowed some feminist claptrap about women's total independence. Such "local" difficulties are not insurmountable given patience, skill and time but keep in mind these are *her* problems, *not* yours. Only take on her baggage if you think there's some hint of mutual attraction. Porters are never happy when they're not tipped.

The true choosy independent, on the other hand, has already met Mr Right; but has also dumped him because she actually prefers to be on her own. She probably still wants sex, and will no doubt get it from time to time but, make no mistake, she is most likely always to keep part of herself distant from any partner.

Please don't be so pompous or misguided as to believe that you will be the one to tame her; any future intimacy is likely to be short-lived.

Dominatrix

Just because you try hard not to control a woman, it doesn't mean you should let her become a control-freak either! The authors find women who only wear bossy boots to be deeply unattractive. Still, there are some women who are just on the dividing line of wanting to dominate and being pleasant to talk to. If you find her attractive, let things run and allow her the edge most of the time. You may well discover that her domineering tendency melts away once she finds out you are man enough to agree when she's right and to call time only when she's wrong.

Arrogant

Self-opinionated and self-focused, she may even go over the top by boasting of her ability to twist men around her little finger.

Deflect her arrogance. Don't let it swamp you. She may, however, also have the skill to reflect your cool once she adjusts to your lack of concern.

If not, find someone who can.

Competitive

Women don't like to sound catty, which is why they are usually more subtle. You need to recognise her motivation:

"She's really nice, isn't she?" (Genuine? Or is this a crafty put-down of the other woman whom she reckons to be no match for herself.). *Answer*: "You both are."

"How old do you think she is?" (Neatly emphasising her own, younger years.) *Answer*: "I can't tell but she looks older than you."

"You only came over to talk to my friend." (Has she picked up a true vibe from you or is this a cover in the same vein as the "really nice" ploy might be?) *Answer*: "You need not put yourself down. It's *you* I want to talk to."

However, her competing with other women is only to be expected. It's when she openly competes with *you* that there might be a problem.

If she's nasty there's no point in carrying on but, as with arrogance, if there's a hint of friendship, your best ploy to developing conversation is likely to be deflection. Here is an example:

Her: Do you always speak out of turn?
You: You mean talk to people. Yes – ever since I was small.
Her: You're out on the pull aren't you?

You: Yes! Is that a problem?
Her: That was a strange thing to say.
You: Life *is* strange, don't you think?

After a few rebounds you can afford to look her in the eyes
and say: "I guessed you were sharp before I came over to talk
to you but I wasn't expecting so much proof!" If she doesn't
want to sign your peace treaty, then her competitiveness is
probably due to core personality and lack of physical attraction rather than mood or front. Time to go.

Shy/Defensive

Shy girls may be very quiet and find it difficult to look you in
the eye, but they will listen. Defensive women are apt to
respond only with suspicion. The basic problem is helping
them relax. You may need any or every skill we've explained
in this book. However, much as we hate to say it, extroverts
and clowns do seem to stimulate these women best, perhaps
because the spotlight remains on the attention-seeker rather
than her.

  With a deeply shy woman, when all else fails, quietly ask
her, "Why are the good-looking women always quiet?" or
even "Are you shy?" Both options look tremendously risky
on paper, but we have found they are fairly successful in
practice. Either can be just the relief-value she needs to open
up. If you are worried about an adverse reaction to whichever
question you decide to put, you can dilute it with a diplomatic
preamble like: "Please don't take this the wrong way . . .".

Mad flirts

These tend to be good-looking because attractive women have
more options to abuse their natural pulling power. A mad flirt
will often talk loosely about sex, exaggerating availability and
try to ensnare you by using a mixture of eye contact, compliments, immediate touching and laughing uproariously at jokes
even *you* didn't think were very funny. This is when your
mental alarm bells should override other urges.

A simple test will reveal true intentions. Move in closer, touch her, even ask her to dance if you can lay on the music, and see if she backs down. If she does, back off; you will almost certainly be best to drop her like a hot potato.

Mad flirts are at their tempting worst on the dance floor, that most sexpectatious of environments. They will often approach you, make and keep eye contact, and copy your dancing – while adding a few moves of their own, just suggestive enough and close enough to relocate your brain from cranium to crotch. Apply the test. If she retreats sharply, she isn't worth more of your time. If she later returns to you or continues dancing near you, cease to show interest – so demonstrating you won't play her games.

CAUTION: HANDLE WITH CARE

When a woman does let you dance close but soon backs off, this doesn't prove she's a mad flirt. The genuine article won't normally let you touch her. More likely is that she is *bona fide* but prefers not to make herself seem easy, and this is the way women are expected to act, after all.

Rough-lover
Sensible women pull their boyfriends away from fights. Rough-lovers *like* their men to get physical. Luckily for us, this type of women finds it hard to conceal her preference. She applauds tough looks, dress and attitudes, loves to stir-up trouble between males, invariably closes in on any violent confrontation, will directly question the masculinity of more gentle men and, most characteristically, will divulge to total strangers the abuse she has witnessed or suffered with other rough-necks. Our advice, whenever you see enough such signs, is walk away. Fast.

The Great Pretenders
As mood and experience are such essential parts of women's personalities, all the above types may interlink. However,

pretentious women are a breed apart. High disposable income is often a trait of pretenders, but their most common characteristics are being both status-obsessed and paranoid of being stereotyped. Thus they immediately crowbar their multifaceted lifestyles into the conversation. She will tell you how she paddled the Amazon in a canoe, that she belongs to a health club so exclusive they have bouncers on the door, that she is a qualified teacher of a dance style that was last in fashion seventy years ago and that her last boyfriend was an Aborigine, Native-American, Puerto-Rican furniture designer. Sneeringly, they mock women with names like Tracey and Sharon – without acknowledging that a down-to-earth background can give the benefits of a solid outlook on life, which they themselves patently lack. Neither do they realise the delicious irony that searching for the latest fashions, following obscure pop groups and being seen at overpriced venues are as much examples of sheep-like conformity as is any nightclub dance around handbags.

In the old days (i.e. before we knew better), we used to suck up to pretenders by acting as if we were impressed with their life stories, or we catered for their obsession with status by showing off around them. Neither method had much success but the problem was when they *did* succeed. To our horror, we found out during relationships with pretenders that they are the least psychologically stable women it will be your misfortune to meet. A wise man once said that "the difficulty in life is choice" and pretenders simply cannot make their minds up. Thus you may become a punchbag for the competitive (self-imposed) stress that pretenders go through as they try to live up to their fronts. You will need to be mentally robust for any ensuing relationship to last with any hope of her growing out of such a personality defect.

CAUTION: HANDLE WITH CARE
Pretenders tend to patronise venues, which, like them, are pricey and pretentious. Hold on though. Non-pretentious women who want a relaxed, comfortable and trouble-free night

out, bathed in a little affluence and "atmosphere", are also to
be found in such places. You just need to spot the difference.

HELPFUL CONVERSATION LINES
When you are flying solo at a crowded venue, you can
reasonably buy a little time with these: if she asks "Where are
your friends?" say "They're avoiding me – probably because
they all owe me money!" Defer "Are you here by yourself?"
with "No, my friend was around but I expect he's talking to
someone". Of course, you absolutely must come clean if you
are alone but you will now be able to choose your moment.
Please resist answering solo questions with admissions like,
"Yes. No one loves me . . ." She may believe you!

Sapphic back-ups
Some women delight in proclaiming that they're lesbians.
Don't be thrown. Don't get carried away. Such immediate
statements of homosexuality are rarely genuine. Women are
aware of the special place that lesbians occupy in the male
psyche. A blasé response reveals a lot about your sexual maturity. You won't know for sure whether she's a lesbian but
indications she is *not* include: she chats with men as well as
women and maintains similar social space during conversation
with either; her admiring glances are reserved for men; you may
see her fired up with other men but not in the same way with any
other woman; she's not dressed in any stereotypical lesbian
manner (something heterosexual women avoid like the plague).
   Stunning looks, by the way, are no guide. Anyway, even if she
is a lesbian, why should that exclude conversation? Or, indeed,
heterosexual friendship? It all helps you cast your net wider.

Her/Them:	We're partners.
You:	What, business partners?
Her:	I'm a lesbian/We're lovers.
You:	I don't blame you, I like women as well (or)
	Oh. What part of Lesbia do you come from?

MISTAKES

It is completely impossible to avoid all verbal foul-ups. The aim is to make fewer and to recover better than the average lothario. There's nothing wrong with apologising if you've really upset her. Otherwise you are nearly always best just to air-brush over your error by changing the subject, or you may leap into the hands of the type of woman who will relish any opportunity to make you squirm.

Alcohol

Dutch courage may be Holland's most famous export, but you don't need us to tell you that alcohol is the arch-enemy of self-control. Cut back your consumption if you want to improve your chances. This doesn't mean going completely dry. What we advise is to pace yourself, *especially once you hit that familiar, light-headed feeling*. After that go for soft drinks, shandies, mixers, drinking slowly and/or saying "No (thank you)". If others rib you, let them drink yours; they're quickly nonplussed by this tactic when you offer your drink and mean it. Harder drinkers (usually) mean well by plying you with alcohol but more astute observers will recognise (albeit quietly to themselves) your strength of character.

Reassurance

Asking for reassurance can become a bad conversational habit. Quell this impulse ("I'm talking rubbish, aren't I?"; "That wasn't funny, was it?", etc) especially among women you don't know.

You can just about re-register on her confidence detector if you manage to tack on a spot of humour: "That was really boring, wasn't it? Tell you what, I'll give you my number and if you ever have trouble sleeping, call me. Mind you (salacious smile), there are other ways I can help you to settle down to sleep".

Clichés

You will be forgiven for a well-timed cliché or two but never pepper your conversation with them. Add new twists if you can: "Here, look after the pennies, while I pay with *your* credit card"; "You can take a horse to water but you can't make it do backstroke".

Include her
We have already stressed how getting carried away with your own opinions is all too easy (particularly when a woman seems to enjoy your lyrical flow) but remains a turn-off in the long run. Steer your content to ask: "What do you think?"; "Do you see where I'm coming from?" and so on. Then shut your trap long enough for her to take up the running.

Sex
Women tend to have a simple rule about *undue* sex talk: namely, the man who starts it is not getting any! You might risk steering a woman into a light-hearted sexually oriented banter, but always let her be the first to make any serious sexual conversation. That way *she* has made the choice and is dictating the pace.

Even then, don't allow hormones or testicular thinking to overwhelm insight. Remember that mad flirts may bring up sex with no intention of turning gesture or words into action, and also that, although women in general are becoming more open about sexual and emotional conversation with strangers, that doesn't mean they're asking you to seduce them; far from it, it's more likely that they wish unconsciously to test your sense of propriety and reserve. Use her signals as well as her words to make your mind up about how much to say so early on.

Typically, mistakes are caused by going beyond mere sexual innuendo but you can at least try and bounce back with: "Well, that's my fantasy. Don't you believe it either"; or "I guess you haven't clicked on that website then".

6

MOVING ON OR MOVING AWAY

Hear the eerie music? You have now entered the friendship zone. This chapter is about knowing when and how to move beyond that, and when not to bother.

Relationships

You don't have to talk about sex in order to be intimate; however, the less direct subject of relationships stimulates emotions and may open up opportunity when the time is ripe. Few conversations cannot be steered towards them. Any of these lines should suit to warm up the theme: *Holidays* – "So, you had a good holiday. Have you ever enjoyed one of those whirlwind holiday romances?" (leaves her space to omit her most recent trip if she so wishes); *Politics* – "Politicians have affairs left, right and centre. What attracts women to them? Is it their lack of influence!?"; *Sports* – "Do you have a sports idol?"; *Show business* – "If your favourite singer started·chatting you up, would you let him buy you a drink?"; *Books* – "Can you read a bonkbuster without laughing?"; *Star signs* – (best only if she starts talking about them) – "Which star sign is most compatible with you?" or (because it doesn't do to challenge her stereotypical assumptions about men *too* much) "Do you really believe that stuff?"; *Friends* – "Isn't it funny the way some friends disappear when they get a new partner?"; *Work* – "Are you for or against romance at work?"

No doubt you can think up many more openers. Avoid talking about your own past relationships and certainly *never* name names. To ask about her is extremely tactless. Let her speak of such matters when or if she wants.

Risking an affair

Let's not be coy here; affairs go on all the time. The only thing stopping her is *her*, so if she shows signs of desire even though she's hitched, it's then a battle between *you* and *your* conscience. Perhaps this starts with how you define "hitched". Nevertheless, how would you feel if you were the deceived partner? If she's flighty with you, who else will be so lucky? Is she too damned independent for you, as perhaps she already is for him? Our advice is instinctual: does whatever she says feel right (leaving aside the fact you may – temporarily – be biased!)? Are you prepared for the (inevitable) flak?

Positive signs

Women signal their feelings and preferences in myriad ways. So keep alert!

Only you – She remains just a little less open, friendly and complimentary with your friends than she is with you. She may rib you in fun, but also drops some genuine physical or character compliments. She may take her time before doing the latter (in which case you've passed her test of assessment). She will also pointedly ignore any distractions from a "Miss Negative".

Mirroring – Sub-conscious mimicking of your movements. She drinks as you drink, she touches her arm as you do, etc. Imitation always was the most sincere form of flattery . . .

Eye contact – She cannot help but maintain it!

Conversation – Chat is two way, lasts longer than ten minutes, and she tries to keep it going during pauses (God bless her!). You can forgive her any reticent start. A shy woman really will appreciate your patience. Decorum insists she hold back from spilling the beans if she has recently split up. (She should know that being too gushy on this score can put you off.) However, the fact that she doesn't mention any partner and doesn't ask about yours may be a positive sign.

Space – She is happy with you in her personal space.

Contact – Some form of bodily contact is maintained or encouraged – a main prelude to mouth manoeuvres. She might invite you to dance, move closer to you, let a touch linger or touch you in a sensitive area. Some analytical men subtly pull away from touches to see if the woman will try to maintain contact. There's no sense to this. She may not have the confidence to follow you, however slight the gap. Continued contact is all the confirmation you need.

Sex – She opens the subject – albeit only with a jokey remark or gesture – during a first meeting.

Neutral and misconstrued signs
Lack of touch – Not all interested women will touch you first.

One-to-one attention – Giving her undivided attention only to the man with whom she is talking is not necessarily negative. It is polite and perhaps indicates pride. Only that person is worthy of her attention for that time. This means you may have to work hard to attract and then hold her attention, if you think she is worth it.

Pupils – Pupil dilation might be a viable sign of interest, but too many variables can cause it: poor light; her spotting a gorgeous hunk behind you; narcotics; and it can be difficult to see. You're better off placing your trust in more obvious signs.

Presumed success – There is a tacit assumption about her manner that admits you are successful with women. She may or may not be phased by this. You *might* have a problem convincing her you're not a womaniser; she *might* have a problem about seeming "easy". All matters for your good judgment.

Walks away – If she walks away after some daft comment of yours – yes, make a mental note of your mistake but it is also possible that she was not interested in you to begin with. Might she just have been waiting for an "out" so as to return to her friends?

Grooming – You may usually count it as a plus if a woman makes self-conscious adjustments to her appearance as conversation develops. However, if her gestures are extravagant or she requires a mirror to preen herself, suspect vanity.

Agony Uncle – Trust is always welcome but when a woman instantly divulges her woes, it's more likely that she is suffering from baggage overload than that she is interested in you.

Negative signs
Many of these are simply opposites of positive vibes.

Space – You keep a respectable distance, but she keeps moving back.

Breaks – She allows herself to be pulled away from conversation with you without saying that she'll return, or just walks off with not so much as a "by-your-leave".

Charming! – You offer well-timed flattery or reassurance and she immediately starts to play games designed to put you down or make you jealous. Perhaps she mistakes kindness for weakness. However, if she continues in an over-competitive stance with mickey-taking or relapses with monosyllabic answers or arm folding, reject her. Clearly she doesn't want you.

YOU DON'T *HAVE* TO CARRY ON TALKING

Leaving an encounter is not just about being able to recognise negative signs or handle rejection. Women are not the only ones to keep talking when the desire is one-sided! Always ask yourself whether you are enjoying the conversation so much that you're prepared to stay rather than circulate and meet more people. Are you prepared to be friends, possibly for ever? Indeed, would you even like to see her again? Stark questions for the heat of the moment, you may feel; however, if you are answering "No", why hang around?

As long as you do so politely, there's no reason why you shouldn't be the first to bring conversation to a close and move on: "I've got to go, otherwise I'll burst . . ."

CONTRADICTION

Some women have a contradictory habit of locking men in the friendship zone with well-meaning comments that also hit the conscience. You must decode the message: is she just testing you, perhaps on the basis that romance ought to be stronger than lust, or does she genuinely mean it?

If her body language belies her words, you might choose to be a little frivolous without leaving her in too much doubt about your intentions. This allows you to gauge her true feelings. Yes, her reaction might be frosty but, equally, it might prove the turning point between listening and kissing. And, if you like her, that's a risk worth taking:

Her: I love talking to a man who doesn't pretend he'd like to get into my underwear.

You: I don't think your underwear would fit me but, be fair to yourself: you *are very* attractive.

Her: You seem so different. Most men are only after one thing.

You: You mean winning the lottery? (pause to smile) Seriously, I do like talking to you but I also find you sexy.

Here's a corker you may well meet, together with a response which should serve you well.

Her: I'd really like to have a friend like you to discuss absolutely *anything* with.

You: Yes, we could each become the other's confidante.

Mean what you say here because there's a risk that this really *is* all she wants. No matter! Few firmer friendships can be formed and neither of you need ever regret having a platonic bond, even for life. And another:

Her: If only I hadn't already met XXXX, you would be in my frame.

You: Thank you! That's bravely put. Well, I wish you both the best and hope that we can all keep in touch.

Again, who knows to what other friendships a platonic bond may lead?

FUTURE CONTACT

Keep things simple. Ask for her number or invite her to join you for some event coming up (which gives you the excuse to need her phone number). Give her your own home phone number in return. Enquire whether she has transport home; then you can offer it or to call a taxi for her – whichever she likes.

If she wriggles out of giving you her number, you may just have to accept that she has good reasons. Should you, by chance, meet again (perhaps at the same, familiar venue), this may change but there's little mileage in betting on it. She may not intend any out-and-out rebuff or may have her own regrets afterward but that's her life – and you have yours to get on with.

Asking her back to your place

The end of a first meeting or first date is hardly the moment to ask her back to your place.

As a general rule, the authors only pop this tricky question when (a) it has already turned into a close encounter of the intimate kind, or (b) she needs somewhere to stay for the night. Two *very* distinct situations.

Usually the question doesn't arrive until much later in a relationship.

If she asks you back first

Even promiscuous women are very selective in this area, because it's not just about sex but about trust as well.

If she gives you this trust, it should never be abused.

If you're not sure you want to go (men can say ''no'' too!) decline politely so as to leave her ego intact: ''I've got to be up early tomorrow'', etc.). If, however, you're simply caught off-guard but still keen, you'll need to cover any hesitancy quickly; otherwise she may become self-conscious.

Even if you spill your drink in surprise, you can bounce back with: "I'm sorry, I was hoping you might suggest that but I wasn't expecting it. Yes, I'd like to . . ."

CAUTION: HANDLE WITH CARE
No matter whose place you're in, no matter how turned on she seemed before you arrived, she may still say no.

Just because she doesn't mind being alone with you, that doesn't mean she wants to, or *has* to go all, or *any* of the way with you. The same applies, of course, to every future occasion.

When you do make a move, always make it slowly, gently and directly. Not only does this appropriate self-control impress a woman, it gives her a chance to push you away gently if she's not inclined.

Should this happen the first time you try, your friendship will remain intact, even if you never become lovers. And, however deflated you may immediately feel, she will respect you in the long term.

Whenever it happens later on – even if your relationship is on the ebb and it seems unlikely that you will remain lovers – this same principle must stand. To behave otherwise, for example, as if your own carnal desire were all that mattered, will destroy your relationship and probably (deservedly) your reputation too.

If you need to dampen such excesses, try imagining that there is a secret camera recording all your activities. In these days of fibre-optic, and CCTV, there very well might be! Make sure any film with your face on it would pass the censors.

GROUP SITUATIONS
Give your undivided attention to one girl at a time. Avoid glancing around or looking over her shoulder, both of which are highly impolite. This will impress others in the party (if that be your intention) far more than any antics you might dream up. If some other woman less well known to you appears to want to close in (on you), you should be able to

assume her interest is natural, but remember, female sharks bite hard too.

Taken away – If the woman you are talking to at a public venue is dragged away by others, don't follow. Unless they leave altogether, you may have another chance. Invariably the "Miss Negative" (see Chapter 3) who scooped her away will be keen to attract the attention of other men to equalise the fact that she herself was not approached before.

If your woman does not share her (friend's) enthusiasm for the new guys on the block, a quick check on her body language should alert you. Then, while little "Miss Negative" is preoccupied, you can move back in.

And this time, apply the principle of Equal Weight from Chapter 1, by letting your woman know you think her friend is rude. Polite women always wonder if life would be easier for them if only they were like their brash friends. However, if you can validate her better character in this way, you will help her stand firm next time.

Loose bonds – Never demean your friends just to impress women. You will – in the wrong way! Equally, avoid excessive displays of male bonding. The supposed solidarity of men is as off-putting to women as female groups are to men.

Couple pressure – If your best mate starts pressing lips with the woman he's chatting up, don't panic. If the woman you chose likes you, then seeing her friend's enjoyment is likely to increase your chances of intimacy, but she'll respect you even more for not making a pressurised move.

All for one – In groups women often seem to go for the same man. If this is not you, just target one of the ones not talking to Mr Popular. She will be grateful for your attention, even if it takes a while for her to stop looking at him . . .

Strong and silent – Some women definitely go for the quieter type. If you have good friends, you can take it in turns to play this part. Be careful though; dominatrix types find this role irresistible, especially if you're a good looker!

Blocking – You can sometimes rescue a friend even when your own conversation with a group member dries up:

You: Can you do me a favour?
Her: Like what?
You: Well, your friend and my friend seem to be getting on, so please don't break it up.
Her: I'm not like that.
You: Some women are ...

Unless she wants to prove herself a hypocrite, your friend's conversation will now be allowed to reach its natural conclusion.

Mixed groups of your friends

Whenever men and women friends meet, provided you are well respected by the women in the group, this increases your chances of dating inside or even outside the group. Don't abuse this respect by showing off. If your status isn't good, work on it. It may prove much harder to change your friends.

KEEP A GOOD MEMORY

Keeping a (*private*) diary to recall meaningful conversations you have specially enjoyed is well worthwhile. Include things such as her name, her looks, what you liked about her, what she liked about you, her job, her hobbies, where you met her. Regardless of a second meeting not being arranged, if you bump into her she will be favourably impressed – even flattered – by your memory.

A diary requires effort, but even if you forget everything else, try and remember her name. One way to help you do this is, when she first tells you, to commit it to memory by imagining it stencilled like a top-secret stamp below a photograph of her face. A visual-link really does seem to work better for us. So why not try this yourself?

The last tip we can give you on how to continue great conversations? Keep starting them.

7

DATING AND CHASING

Now the real fun starts. You may dream you have found the one for you but be realistic; the divide between winning and losing is still jacked just wide enough for your ego to drop straight through. You won't easily close this gap unless you continue to *respect her*, and all the basic principles that make really good relationships so precious.

TELEPHONING

Exchange of numbers may seem like a mini-victory at the time but don't get too excited. A few women proffer false numbers rather than appear rude. Others may have very sensible reasons for this deception as we have outlined previously. A final minority may choose to be difficult because that's just the way they are! You won't be the first man to be perplexed and disappointed by false digits so don't take it too personally if it happens.

Never *expect* her to call, no matter what she may have seemed to promise. Most women don't like to call for fear of appearing too keen but this doesn't mean that they are not interested.

As intimidating as it can be, you just need to accept that you will normally have to call first.

If she *does* phone you, and you are interested, play it cool, but not freezing. Let her know that you're flattered by her interest:

Her: Hello, can I speak to Peter?

Him: Peter speaking.

Her: Hi. Do you know who this is?

Him: I think so, but this is the first time I've heard your voice on the phone. Is it Tracy?

Her: You don't sound so sure! Do you get lots of women phoning you?

Him: No, which is why it is nice to hear from you. How are you?

Her: I'm fine. Are you surprised I phoned?

Him: No. I'm glad and delighted you remembered.

Her: I know but women don't normally phone guys . . .

Him: Oh, well, I don't go in for all that old-fashioned stuff. *I* like surprises. So, what have you been up to since we last spoke . . .?

When to call?

We wouldn't leave it longer than a week after getting her number. Longer simply risks her meeting someone else a little quicker off the mark. Preferably you should call after the third day. Any sooner and she may worry that you're too keen. However, if you gave her a specific earlier or later time when you would call, then stick to it. Her positive assumptions of you being trustworthy and interested will outweigh any supposed negative assumptions of your being predictable or soft. As a general rule, you will find it safer to ward off such worries by not being so precise.

If she's out but you are able to speak to someone, or you reach a machine, always leave your name and number. Give your first name and surname in the first instance – especially if your first name (or nickname) is a very popular one. If she doesn't call back, give her no more than a couple more tries (perhaps spaced over time to allow for the possibility of her being away).

After that, if your messages draw no response, STOP! The appropriate words then – are "dead", "flogging" and

"horse". The only exception might be if a game of telephone-
tag developed – with plausible reasons combined with positive,
encouraging messages reaching you via her flatmate, or one of
yours, or on your own answerphone, e-mail or whatever.

What to say
This is where your diary of meaningful encounters can come
in handy; so that you can pick up on such matters as her likes
and dislikes, her favourite topics, or perhaps refer back to
some significant incident that happened when you met. Have
your "crib-sheet" ready when you phone. You may not need
it and we don't especially encourage planned scripts because
you can't predict what she'll say – but – you'll definitely bless
it if you hit any tricky, blank pauses.

It's also important to be prepared for the dreaded answerphone. Hi-tech call-back systems reveal if you've rung a
couple of times without leaving a message and this may send
out an unintentionally negative feel to your subsequent call. A
clear, first-time answerphone message commands respect.
You are probably best to strike a brief, friendly tone the first
time you ring: "This is XXX XXXXX calling at [time] on
[day] the [date]. My number is XXXXXX. I hope you've been
having fun since we met at [place] and I would like to talk to
you soon." There's no need to ask her to phone you. Her good
manners should take care of that.

How long to talk for?
Please avoid the very male mistake of telling her you haven't
got time to talk as soon as she answers the phone! Set aside at
least a half hour, even if you don't expect to use it all. Try to
break off once you've fixed a date but without seeming abrupt.
Keep a few spare arrows back in your quiver.

Making the move for the date
Listen *carefully*. Does she sound pleased to have your call or
is her tone sometimes gritty? If the whole conversation is fun,
you're probably home and dry. Just to make sure, ask for your

date after she has shared a laugh with you.

If you're getting the feeling she's uncomfortable, you need to ask some *defining* questions such as: ''You don't sound too happy. What's up?'' rather than encouraging rejection with a weak ''Aren't you happy to hear from me?'' Why make it easy? You had the courage to call; the least she can do is to be honest about how she feels.

Unless she makes clear she doesn't want to see you again, try for your date. After all, her negativity may only be founded on assumptions and you can always prove these wrong.

Be assertive when you make the move. Choose: ''Would you like to come on a riverboat trip?'' (i.e. be specific) rather than: ''So, when should we meet up?'' Having some alternatives in mind will save you from the unexpected: ''I've just been there and got the T-shirt!''

Dead-end resistance

Outright rejection: ''Oh no, not you!'' is bound to hurt but accepting it at once stems the pain and should prevent you blurting out something you may, one day, much regret. Who knows in what circumstances you might meet again? Just thank her for being straightforward and say your goodbye.

Other rejections you should not force are ''I'm sober now'', ''I'm flat out this summer and, after that, I'll need a rest!'' and the classic ''Let's just be friends''. The latter is often under-rated, however, if she says it *before* you've even made your move then you have to take it seriously. Otherwise it's important to understand that women who like to take things very slowly know that they can't play with a man's heart like a tennis ball, and that this can be one way to ensure your company without leading you on unduly:

Her: I'm not sure it would be a good idea for us to meet up.
You: Why, what's wrong?
Her: Well, I don't want a relationship right now.

You: I appreciate that, but I'm not asking for one. I'm happy just to go out and have a good time. At least then we'll know a bit more about each other before going our separate ways.

Her: Okay, but please can we definitely make this just as friends?

Her setting the parameters like this may only be meant as a springboard for you to deny your instant attraction if she's not ready to admit hers. However, you may be able to fast-forward a little here, the better to judge her real feelings for you. At least she's agreed to meet.

So, instead of responding ''Sure thing'', play by her rules. Come back with a more honest:

You: (thoughtfully) I was going to play this smooth but I'd rather say how my hopes are running even though I'm prepared just to be friends at the moment.
You're probably right to be worried because I *would* like to be more than just friends in the long run.

Her: That's what made me so cautious . . .

You: Hold on. Is it such a bad thing that I find you attractive?

Her: No. I like you, but, like I said, I'm just not ready for a relationship.

You: And you're positive about that?

Her: Yes. I'm sorry.

You: Well, this is hard for me. I don't want to lose touch with you, but I need some time to adjust to this idea of just being friends. Is it okay if I call you in a while?

If she says yes, you may be in for a very long haul but you will have to abide by your promises unless or until she softens her shell – because those are the only conditions in which she might do so. You'll just have to decide whether and for how long you can afford to stay this course.

Where to go?
Women are notoriously indecisive on this, which is why we suggested having some ideas of your own at the ready. Offer a choice, if possible, and flexibility to incorporate her suggestions too. Most women appreciate playing their part.

Pick-up joints, where you first met, anywhere laddish and noisy or where your friends will be, are unlikely to be suitable. Women can be incredibly paranoid about being paraded and do not appreciate being used as an ego boost. Introducing her to your closest friends is another matter, but still generally to be enjoyed later, by and by, and when she is happily more intimate with you.

If you do decide to introduce a new girlfriend to the fold, she will naturally want to make a good impression as will your friends. The atmosphere thus will be conducive to her getting to know you, relaxed from the pressures of a one-to-one situation.

By the way, make the best of your extra freedoms here. Work your introductions. Don't wait to be introduced. Always take time out to talk with your other friends and couples along the way so that your hoped-for dating plans don't look too obvious. Of course, you must trust her not to run off with any of your friends and you must be loyal enough not to chat up anyone else in front of her.

Whatever the supposed main highlight of your first date may be, don't lose sight of the need for quality time together, without distraction. Make it just you and her at least for some of the time, for example, by including going for a walk, a country drive, or perhaps visiting a gallery or museum.

Going to a cinema does not allow much talking time but, if you do agree on it, play safe with a feel-good movie or comedy.

What if a man answers the phone?
Take this in your stride. Acting suspicious won't endear you to anyone. He is probably her flat-mate, brother or a visiting friend. However, if *he* gets heavy, put the phone down and

forget her. You don't want to be a pawn in her game.

(Incidentally, if *she* answers but sounds subdued or hurried or you can hear a man in the background, you may need to treat what she actually says rather like a coded message. She may want to see you as much as you'd like to see her but needs time to unravel her love-life a little first. A little tact and patience now may go a long way.)

YOUR FIRST MOVE

First date nerves

She will probably need relaxing as much as you do. In our male-oriented society, the onus remains on you to provide the necessary mellow vibes. Moderate nervous tension is entirely normal for either of you. Hyper-stress is not fatal either; it abates quickly once you can help each other laugh about it all. Lower your expectations by focusing on any of these which apply:

* Simple friendship is plenty for starters.
* She may be on the rebound, unable yet to devote her full attention to you.
* She may have a partner she wants to leave but still needs to be eased out of her situation.
* Natural female reluctance is in play lest she appear too easy.
* She may not be the person you had on your pedestal.
* She may want to hold back a little after a whirlwind first contact.
* You had to work so hard to get the date, you can hardly expect instant compatibility.
* She was a little tipsy when you first met.
* It's a blind date.

Concentrate on the job in hand. Whatever the butterflies may be doing in your stomach, smile when you greet her. Unless you are being introduced for the first time by mutual friends or have perhaps been put in touch via a dating agency, why not kiss her on the cheek? The kiss is not essential but both actions will establish warmth and confidence on your part, while making her feel desired. You can bet she's spent time dolling herself up for you so be sure to compliment her on how good she looks as well.

Ask her how she is but don't react in any way huffily if she seems negative. Her blues may be nothing to do with you. Just show your concern and share the hope that whatever may be troubling her will pass off quickly. Later, if her mood doesn't seem to be lifting, you could suggest her going home and the possibility of another date. Take it all at face value unless she makes it extremely obvious she wishes she had never accepted your date.

Punctuality
Be on time, not on her nerves! If something goes wrong at the last minute to make you held up, immediately let her know, if you possibly can, that you may be late. Etiquette decrees that she is allowed to be a little late so there's nothing to get fussed about unless this is an extreme half hour plus. Then, if she doesn't apologise, you've got your answer!

Be prepared to be stood up
If she is not there or hasn't turned up after half-an-hour, ring her. If that indicates she is out, check back home, if you can, to see if she's rung you. If all that draws a blank, you must decide how long it is reasonable to wait. This will depend on whether she might have missed a connection, broken down or whatever and perhaps on whether you are now able to leave a fresh message she will certainly get. An hour should be plenty before giving up. If you know a message will have reached her, you can await developments. Otherwise, ring her next day but don't count on hearing what you want to hear!

Preparations
Make an effort to look good and, if it's a second meeting, don't wear the same clothes.

If you don't date much, for example, or are not sure on matters of dining etiquette, glance through a couple of suitable books or take a good friend to one side and ask what you need to know. It might even help to visit the venue with your friend beforehand.

The money
Plenty of girls nowadays may have more immediate cash flow than you have yourself. Nonetheless, it remains usual for the person who asks for a first date to pay, so you need to be ready to cover the finances. Fortunately, when the bill comes, a woman will often offer to meet you halfway and you need not feel bad about accepting. (This *may* be why she insisted on going somewhere inexpensive – but don't count on her loose change!)

Despite our comments about the superficials in Chapter 1, money isn't everything – even if you've not got much! Stigma has largely gone out of the window here and women do understand, for example, when a man (especially while still young) has not yet reached his full earning potential. The key thing is to establish boundaries early if you need to. Be as direct as you can. Dropping what [only] you see as hints can lead to misunderstandings. If she decides she wants to go somewhere expensive, be up front: "I'd love to but I cannot afford to go there". Her reaction will show you her true attitude to money.

Caution about a money-grasping nature is always advisable but do keep a sense of balance. The boot could be on the other foot. If she's been out of work, has family to keep, or is a student, for example, you might be surprised how many stingy men she's met who still expect her to pay her way. Easing the way for a financially-challenged woman is an area for judgment and mutual respect.

The chat
Thinking too hard *in advance* about what to talk about can be counter-productive. Take encouragement from the fact that

you need to talk *with* her, not *at* her – so you will be sharing the pleasures of making conversation as well as the relaxation of silences enjoyed together. There's no need to stress yourself witless! Nonetheless, try to retain and maintain some good anecdotes on which to draw (this becomes a way of life before you know it), and be ready with some newsy items you feel she will be interested to hear.

Any one-to-one date is a golden opportunity to gain trust with your genuine honesty. As a guide, the less she opens up, the more you should be prepared to give. Small snippets of vulnerability prefaced by "I don't usually tell people this but . . ." may add a touch of intrigue but don't overdo them.

You may find that you can go beyond listening. For instance, if she now trusts you with her problems, she probably respects you enough to accept any advice you have; so don't be shy of diplomatic firmness.

"Well, if I was getting bullied at work like you, I'd start keeping a diary of incidents, as well as trying to get a new job, but I guess doing it is easier than it sounds . . ."

"I see. You said you've been together for a long time and I'm no saint, but the reason he keeps cheating on you is perhaps because you let him . . ."

"Yes. It is hard making new friends nowadays and you've known her for a long time but, if she keeps trying to put you down, maybe she's not a true friend after all?"

"I've got no idea what the full story is between you and your mum but, if not talking hurts you this much, maybe you'll just have to be brave and get in touch with her."

How is it going?
We offer the following to help tune your antennae:

Good signs
She's happy to pay her way; opens up plenty more; talks about you and the future in the same breath; allows/initiates more physical contact; wants to know about you; listens intently.

Bad signs

Her conversation centres around money and material com-
forts; she is rude to people serving her, such as waiters,
telephonists, cashiers, etc. (a firm but tactful request may be
reasonable; a sarcastic demeaning rebuke, however, is not on);
she talks with fond nostalgia of horrendous past boyfriends
(her still wanting a man who has treated her badly makes you
wonder quite what she is after); she constantly competes with
and interrupts you; you get the strong feeling you can't even
be 75% of yourself with her around or that it would be hard to
admit any of your weaknesses.

DATING DILEMMAS

Serial dating

Yes, dating consumes time and money and it can be severely
emotionally draining, especially each time the realisation sinks
in that you and the woman aren't compatible. However,
experiences gained from one-to-one meeting are rarely wasted
as we could testify were this book to be ten times longer! Just
enjoy the ride until you find yourself swept along. Then it
might be serious . . .

"To be or not to be" – intimate, that is

On your first date whether to offer (or receive!) that first kiss
is all about how you click. If her signals are strong, you
probably won't feel reticent either. Usually, however, it will
take a couple of dates (or more) before you both feel ready.
Suppose you've had a date or two and little or nothing has
happened, but interest is mutual and you've agreed to meet
again. You can take it the chase is definitely on, so why force
the issue?

   As you begin to see her more often, don't fret but do try to
sense when the moment is ripe. At the end of an evening, before
you part, is traditional but you may feel it wise, given her
unique personality, to choose some less conventional moment –
perhaps, for example, when her smile gives away her desire.

The main thing we must emphasise, however, is not how to pick up positive signs but how to *recognise negative ones*, those intended to preserve her reserve for a little longer or perhaps for always. She may not actually be sure yet how she truly feels about you anyway.

If most of her significant cluster (see page 53) signs are negative, you can be certain the wisest move is not to make a move.

Nerves may afflict you, even when you're convinced she's attracted to you. If so, just make the move in the manner advised on page 143, rather than searching desperately for soothing words or noises to prime her. Wait perhaps until you're saying goodnight and then kiss her gently and slowly on the cheek. If she offers you her lips or lingers in return, then you may not part for a while longer!

If instead she pulls back or quickly turns her head, just murmur that ''that's okay'' or something similar; reverse engines on this score for the rest of the evening concerned. If it's nothing, you'll know soon enough when you next see her. If it's important, your patience should be rewarded. If you never see her again, well, there's your answer!

THE CHASE
During early days in a budding romance, game-playing rules OK. It may be teasing; it may be defensive; but it's certainly allowed. You may even indulge yourself though we're not recommending some complex strategy!

The important thing to realise is that, if she sometimes seems to be buying time, that's probably all she *is* doing. You need not begin harbouring huge reservations about her underlying character.

Ring-me
She likes you enough to continue seeing you, but that doesn't mean she wants you to ring her all the time. Indeed, if you can manage a degree of unpredictability about when or how often you ring, you will reduce any feeling of pressure from her

point of view. This can also make her more delighted when you do ring. (Remember, you may have the rest of a lifetime to prove steady and reliable about your every movement . . .)

I-won't-be-around

You naughty little stopout! More seriously, you're entitled to your space and shouldn't feel the need to explain away every evening of snooker or going to football with your friends, etc. If the relationship blossoms, you will bless having established with her that you need some freedom. She will assuredly need hers too. Play this one sparingly though. You won't be wanting a partner you never see!

Not too single

Despite the undoubted status of partnered men, single women do actually prefer single men. But not *too* single. The trouble is, women are very talented anglers when fishing for the truth. You may need to embellish that truth a little in the face of awkwardly accurate leading questions. An alternative is to exaggerate your answers. For example, to "What films have you seen recently?" list off as many as you can remember. To "Do you like skiing?" mention all the women you've ever met in the mountains even if they weren't on your party. No need to say you've been three times unless she asks and no need to specify relationships. Let her decide what "I went with Denise and Roger" might, or might not, mean.

Drop everything

This play is triggered when she calls early one evening, unexpectedly, and wants company. You can afford to show a smidgeon of reluctance, even if you were re-reading the TV schedules. Otherwise her instant gratitude will tend to give way to feelings of vague contempt for your "too eager to please" nature. Suggest you were going to do some DIY, go training, or whatever might have been in character for you but there's no necessity to disappoint:

Her: My tennis has been cancelled and I was wondering if you want to go out later?

You: Well, I had XXXXX in mind to do and I must finish YYYY. What were you thinking?

Her: Well, I just thought maybe you'd like to see that film we talked about.

You: Hmm. I can be through doing YYYY by (time) and XXXXX could wait until next week. Is it okay if we go to the late-night viewing?

Her: Yes, but look, if you'd rather go another night . . .

Him: No. I want to see you. Let's meet at 9.45 pm at our usual spot outside the multiplex.

Hopefully this "gamesmanship" stage will be short-lived and playful rather than hurtful. Then you can concentrate on continuing a satisfying relationship.

Friends

It's always a good sign if she seems eager to introduce you to her friends. In their company just be yourself: don't even think of trying to look casual, still less to impress. Unseemly attention given to any of her girlfriends won't be her idea of fun, either, even if you are known for being an outrageous tease or the girl in question to be a mad flirt.

Gifts

The romance of intimate gifts lies in their personal nature. Surprise is more important than extravagance, which can embarrass and perhaps cause her to wonder about either your self-confidence or even your motive. Such kindness is usually best left until intimacy has truly developed. However, there is here a wide spectrum to be governed by appropriateness as well as good taste and individual circumstances. We would suggest, *certainly to begin with*, and for quite a long time thereafter (unless engagement suddenly appears on the cards) that simply giving her your time, paying your way on dates and letting her know that you like her, is the right approach.

The temptation is to go over the top, particularly if you see signs or hear tales of lavish gifts from others. If you do get expensive and she then spurns your company, don't blame this book!

Even Christmas and birthdays are better kept low-key when you haven't known each other long. A nice card and flowers may be quite enough. It's the thought (and remembering!) that counts.

Letters can be very romantic if you are a good writer. Take care, though, about the meaning and strength of what you write because breaking up might otherwise become ever harder to do!

Generally, we favour the directness of spoken words; however, if either of you travel a lot or circumstances force you apart for weeks or months, letters may come into their own – especially as you can now choose to despatch and receive them with the speed of e-mail.

She's coming over
At the risk of sounding like nannies, we offer some advice that should go without saying!

You may not have much control over flatmates but *she will notice* if your place doesn't seem clean and fresh. So tidy up.

Clear all washing up from the kitchen; hoover and dust and try to air these rooms if you can. Your own room should reflect well the standards you like to keep, so change the linen if it's due, dust, clean, put away clothes and do whatever else may be necessary. Don't forget to make sure bathroom and loo are immaculate, with fresh handtowels, soap and so forth available.

And by the way, throw out non-educational media that has, as they say in the trade, "a high-skin quotient". Finally . . . hide this book!

Finishing lines
She may give little away that tells you where you stand. Choice, fear, upbringing, inexperience, all manner of reasons can cause her to hold back; she may not even be sure quite what drives her actions at the moment.

You may suffer some mixed feelings yourself as time slips remorselessly by.

Either way, if this sort of uncertainty begins to prevail, doubt is likely to creep in around the edges of your psyche and it is time to clear things together, things perhaps unspoken of between you until now.

Logically, the Chase mode should not last forever, but then neither should its duration be governed by any preordained rules. So the timing of true intention must come from one of you. As usual it will probably have to be you.

You need to prick the uncertainty.

These preambles should ease you gently in to the subject so that meaningful answers can flow more freely:

"Would you, as Minister for Home Affairs, like to tell me whether I'm right to have become so fond of you?"; "I like you as more than a friend but I'd love to know, well, just how you like me?"; "Before you become my significant "other", I feel we need to talk a little."

The clock of pursuit is then set by her reaction. Here is a more complex reaction where some perseverence and patience are surely in order:

Her: I don't want to get involved again so soon after my bust-up.

You: I understand. (pause) I hope I would never hurt you like he did.

Her: He said something like that too. You men are so predictable!

You: (quietly but firmly) That's wrong, you know.

Her: All right, but you have no idea what I'm really like.

(If this is a prelude to sharing where she feels she went wrong, then *maybe* she is prepared to change.)

You: I like the you I know so far and I'm willing to deal with the rest as it comes up. I'm not perfect so I definitely don't expect you to be.

In general, hesitancy, wavering or being vague mean she's still some way behind you in terms of any commitment. If you can bear it, let matters hang there. She's on notice. She'll tell you in her own way when she's ready – provided you can give her space and time to make up her mind.

Conversely, you may just have to come to terms with a blunt rejection. These examples should be pretty clear:

* "I'm a lesbian" (and you are sure she's lying).

* "I must explain about my boyfriend."

* "You're a nice guy but . . ." (No buts; you're too nice for her.)

* "We've got nothing in common." (She's *decided*!)

We regard rejection which pre-empts your expression of desire as generally too fixed to hope for change.

You: I've got to tell you something –
Her: Don't say it.

If you decide to carry on chasing, good luck! You may be on your own . . .

She may be open with you first. She may or may not manage to be polite or to choose her words carefully. You may have trouble with the shock and the let-down, but be brave through those emotions for both your sakes. Her decision is clear. Pleading or battle now won't help either of you.

Her: I know how much you like me, but I'm afraid I just don't seem to feel the same way for you.
You: I'm glad you've felt able to say this now. You've set both of us free and I will always respect that.

You've set the tone for letting go – swift action that will bring comfort and relief both to her and you.

Keeping in contact

Suppose for the next few paragraphs that your relationship is going through a "down". The Chase has cooled. You are aware that she wants time to think. She may perhaps have said, "Can we just be friends at the moment?" or her current vibes set alarm bells jangling too often for your piece of mind.

This state of play is par for the course! Although we know it doesn't help you to tell you this now!

You are going to have to make up *your* mind whether there is hope and how you are going to run your life while waiting, or whether the relationship really *is* over.

The latter, excruciating as it may be whilst the reality sets in, is easier. Small comfort but we hope you both manage to emerge with your dignities unscathed and able to remain friends even at a respectable distance.

The former position of hope, when you honestly believe things could still go either way, may be likened to a period of slow torture. It is definitely the time when she is most in control of the Chase and you will need your wits about you while you have little choice but to bide your time.

Provided she has left the door ajar, there's nothing wrong with continuing to meet. Just don't swamp her. Make an effort not to call her or see her so much. If she cares enough, she will probably contact you. If she asks why you haven't phoned, just imply that you've been busy. If she asks you out, accept. When you meet, don't be stand-offish, give her a hard time or be the first to bring up the subject of your overture. Simply be affectionate, complimentary and assertive when it's appropriate.

If she seems to prefer seeing you only in the company of other friends, don't put her off. Just go along with this for the while. She may seem to have taken charge but that's not always a bad thing. Feeling powerful can make even shy women bold enough to be direct. If the good signs begin to sideline bad ones, you may just be getting something right together . . . There's no need to seize back the initiative for the sake of macho pride. Control-freaks don't make good lovers anyway. Equality and sharing [decisions] are the things that will help her flourish. Here are some more clues:

Positive signs
She turns to you in time of crisis; touches you more; phones often and initiates meetings; doesn't repeat that she wants a platonic relationship; praises you, even in front of others; doesn't encourage other men when you're around; invites you round or is willing to visit your home.

Negative signs
Tend to be opposites of positive ones: she only calls *after* you do; a trusted source tells you that she has been running you down behind your back; she continues to keep her feelings to herself; she talks about her past partners repetitiously. If you don't like this last indulgence, now's the time to tell her. She may not be aware it's annoying you but, once told, she will probably respect your feelings and it may help her to stop comparing you so much in ways that may be unconsciously destructive.

We wish you every luck sorting out such clues and hope we have been able to help you cherish good luck or diminish pain.

Friendship
Even when a relationship is over, friendship should remain your goal. You may not ever see each other again, or not for some while, but there is little purpose in either of you storming off leaving a bad taste all round. You can tell female friends things you can't tell men and they can give you a direct insight into female nature. The authors have had some fantastic wholly platonic relationships with women, as well as some which have evolved as such and we wouldn't change them for *anything*.

However, staying friends after feelings have been declared may require a mammoth maturity that, only too late, you realise you don't have. There is always the risk of fall-out of atomic proportions as you magnify in your mind every missed

date, every sign of interest in another man and every unfulfilled favour into a malicious abuse of power. When you
constantly want to phone her, always wonder what she's
doing, fume if she doesn't contact you, negatively compare
her to all other women and, most importantly, when she has
made it clear that she doesn't want you like you want her;
don't delude yourself. It's not love; *it's obsession*. It can be a
frighteningly easy state of mind to slip into, especially if she is
everything you believe her to be, but it only ever ends in tears.
The obsessed man must realise that continued pursuit will only
reinforce her negativity, as well as risking running himself
into the ground. Not loving you equally may or may not be her
problem but don't allow stratospheric pride or, conversely,
low self-esteem to make it yours too. In the last resort, try
these infatuation reducers:

* Go on holiday away from her.
* Avoid being where you know she is going to be.
* Lose her contact numbers.
* Talk to friends. Ask their honest advice. Listen.
* Seek counselling. See your doctor if you are becoming
  depressed.

Single mothers
You may not know all her circumstances when you first meet.
Second encounters are a different matter. If you don't have
children and have never been out with a single mother before,
your first impulse may be to run. Hang on, though. She may
have brought up the children alone perfectly successfully for
some while. There's no need automatically to assume she's
looking for a father figure.

Your relationship with her children will be important,
obviously, more so the younger they are. At only a few years
of age, they will be developing fast, even though probably
unaware of the full implications of your relationship. Yet you
can easily find they challenge your role, steal your fire and
make you feel like an intruder with the minimum of effort.

The remedy is to show the same respect for them as you do for her. Only that genuine recognition will help them feel less threatened and you will hopefully be rewarded for your concern.

You have a duty to be very self-aware here. You don't have to feel guilty if you're not ready for the responsibilities of a step-father, but you must always be honest about your feelings. Otherwise those children can all too easily get hurt. That's why showing equal respect for the family as a whole is paramount.

8

FIRST-TIME SEX

The notion that Safe Sex exists defies belief, dismissing as it does all the lessons of history and all the damage irresponsibility can and does cause.

Chapter 2 and much else in this book have asked you to face these real issues.

This chapter begins by trusting that you have done so and are therefore free to focus on sexual union itself, the thrill of thrills, with all its potential for deepening your relationship.

The hugs, kisses, sighs and moans have gone as far as clothes will allow, and both of you are ready for what will assuredly be a crucial step. Yet, even in this high-octane state of expectation, you may be aware of certain nagging feelings, tugging like an irritating child at the sleeves of your mind.

Your nerves are not unique. Even successful sexanovas worry about their first-time performance. Frequent sex doesn't mean it's good or that he is impervious to self-doubt. Starting-block anxieties such as ''I hope I don't finish too soon'' or ''I hope she doesn't think I'm small'' are commonplace. Other fears, such as worries about hairy backs or knobbly knees, are more personal. However, one thing is for sure: without confronting any sexual fears you might have head-on, you will not find full sexual enjoyment and neither will any prospective partner.

THE BIG "O"

For all but the most selfish of men, adequacy of performance is tied to the male ego as securely as his need for love itself. Such male pride that your lovemaking skills will take her to a la-la land of sexual arousal where her orgasm matches the spectacle and power of an erupting volcano is, however, all too often misplaced. There's no question that being the sole cause of such pleasure for both of you is the right target but the brutal truth is that you are still more likely to achieve orgasm during sexual intercourse than she is. Research suggests that as many as a quarter of women in established relationships have yet to achieve an orgasm with their partner. In a survey of 20,000 adults interviewed in the UK, over 48% of men and 43% of women held the view that sexual satisfaction for men could not be achieved without an orgasm. In contrast, only 37% of men and 28% of women thought that sex without orgasm for the woman would not be satisfying. So, if the learning curve takes time, and lots of it, you will not be alone.

Although recent research suggests that the female climax raises the chances of conception, it is ejaculation that is necessary for the survival of the species. Who knows? Perhaps it is to this end that a woman's arousal is usually slower than is a man's and that her major erogenous zone (the clitoris) is not as well-placed as yours (have a guess) to achieve orgasm from penetrative sex.

Of course, nature is not totally unsympathetic to the female. Intercourse is pleasing and desirable for women (otherwise they wouldn't indulge and then where would men be?) but penetration alone is unlikely to ring the chimes in her belfry. When you throw the importance of other factors, such as compatibility, guilt and experience into the mix of first-time sex, it's no wonder that it doesn't always live up to expectations.

Just as with a failed chat-up line, her lack of orgasm, if it doesn't happen, is never *entirely* the man's fault, but expecting too much is. Adult women know the difference between good and bad sex, regardless of climax. So don't make the mistake of unwarranted optimism. Your sexual success depends above all on having the right attitude.

Having made these points, it should be clear that both of you may need great love, care and patience with your sex lives. There can be few parts of life in which you can help each other more through good communication. If success still evades you several months down the line, it may be time to refer to books, many can be very helpful but be sure to compare several so as to feel comfortable that they make sense to you. (Regrettably, chicanery and sensationalism pervade some such tomes in the hope of selling more – whereas you probably want simple, sane advice.) Next stop, if you still have problems, should be the medical profession, starting with your own doctors.

ATTITUDE
Today's permissive media swamp people with data on sexual technique and practices. In its most vulgar forms, close to or actual pornography, it would seem that a touch here, a lick there and, supposedly, she'll be begging you for regular sex. Hardly any of this matches reality, still less allows for the innumerable individual differences between women, and only the most perceptive of men might get an inkling of what a potential lover will be like when the lights go out.

Cutting through all this "noise" only one attribute really counts. You have to be willing. Willing to:

* Pleasure a woman
* Listen and learn
* Ask for what you want
* Let yourself go.

Pleasuring
Pleasuring her does not universally mean orgasm, either for her or even necessarily for you. It simply means showing her that your aim is mutual satisfaction. The key word women use

is "consideration", and it's as good a description as any other. Take your time with foreplay. Patience is the key virtue which will pay dividends to the man who can show a capacity for selfless lovemaking.

Asking, listening and learning

The second and third aspects of willingness are harder to fulfil during first-time sex, because you may not be comfortable enough yet to tell each other just what you want. You must tune yourself to her body language. When she shrinks away from a certain touch, try somewhere else. When she nudges you in a certain direction, follow her lead. Film fantasy consistently belies first-time reality. Whether the film comes from Hollywood or back street Soho, celluloid women are always eager to please and penetratively multi-orgasmic. Back on terra firma, women take time, men are still expected to initiate certain actions and one orgasm intercourse is a rare enough beast, never mind several times over. In this conflicting climate, the importance of good verbal and physical communication cannot be overstated.

As you get to know each other more, there may come times when you crave relief from ecstasy yet, for example, she is not so far down her similar track of excitement or perhaps not wishing to be so for the moment. One possibility is that you could then take matters in to your own (ahem), or rather her, hands. However, despite increasing media attention on bedroom equality, you'll probably find that you have to give oral sex or stimulate her by masturbation before she will reciprocate.

Letting go

It's hard to be an atheist when you're having an orgasm. Men tend to want to believe the "Oh God" factor from women so much that it can also blind them to another aspect of women's reticence which can be surmised from the orgasm statistics above. Women like to make men climax. The male orgasm makes her feel special because she, and only she, has taken you to this most vulnerable, most open state. So, when your love-train is pulling in to Nirvana station, don't be shy of announcing it on the tannoy. We're not advocating faking it (though you wouldn't be the first!); just go with the flow of your emotions. Cut through that natural male reserve which mistakenly makes you think that you should always be in control. What are you worried about? That she might laugh? Such laughter is just a nervous reaction anyway, possibly because so many men keep the lid on their feelings even in this highly emotional state. Even if you're the type of man who sheds a tear at the critical moment, you will find that, provided you're not a wet blanket out of bed, women are more likely to find this endearing than off-putting.

SAFETY FIRST

All sexual encounters carry the risk of unwanted pregnancy. In Chapter 2 we have urged that you THINK and DISCUSS *before* you act. Procreation and recreation have ever sat uncomfortably close here and this possible consequence dare not be ignored – more especially if it is only for the sake of some fling or holiday madness.

Have you thought through what psychological impact an abortion might have on either of you or, indeed, on other members of your family? Have you considered the long term needs of a child born to you both? Can you carry such responsibilities for the rest of your lives?

Unfortunately, you need to know the answers now.

Contraception

You do need to be aware that no form of contraceptive, other than the simple word "no" is 100% effective.

Pregnancy risk rates for the various contraceptive methods are widely quoted but few partners seem fully to understand also that vigorous sperm can reach the tip of the penis well before ejaculation, swimming their way upward via the mucus secretion of its Cowper's gland. It should not require too much imagination to appreciate how little further bodily fluid may be needed for them to make their way right up the vagina even without actual penetration. This is one reason why coitus interruptus, apart from any other disadvantages it may have, should be ruled out in the majority of situations.

Inevitably (sadly) the risk of disease has to be faced. You are probably aware of long-standing sexually-transmitted diseases like genital herpes, gonorrhoea, serum hepatitis, and syphilis. All these diseases should be taken seriously but by far the worst is the dreaded HIV virus. The consequences of catching HIV are enough to make the most staunch naturalist convert to man-made protection. Though the most ominous predictions of the early eighties have not materialised in many countries including Britain (perhaps all the warnings worked after all; while improved medication has enabled people to live longer with the disease), *don't be lulled into a false sense of security*. The number of HIV cases here in Britain has still risen each year since records began in 1982. AIDS remains incurable.

Luckily, with HIV, following some simple steps should limit the transmission risk. These same precautions should also help prevent other sexual diseases.

Safe steps
Always use a condom for any type of genital contact that involves exchanging bodily fluids.

We suggest that you use sheaths that are treated with non-oxynal 9, a spermicide thought (but only from the results of laboratory testing) to be effective in neutralizing HIV.

When using rubber condoms, only use water-based lubricants, such as KY jelly. Oil-based lubrication can degrade rubber sheaths. A polyurethane (plastic) condom is now on the market which can be used with both oil- and water-based lubricants, but always check the packet instructions.

Avoid oral sex if you have a mouth ulcer, bleeding gums, cut lips, etc.

Put more emphasis on low-risk activities, such as mutual masturbation, kissing and foreplay.

Practise condom use with or without your partner.

Have any genital infection treated as soon as it appears. Symptoms may disappear soon after first showing but this *doesn't always mean the infection has gone*.

Due to the penetrative nature of male sexuality, your main focus in terms of disease must be on condom-protected sex. Never rely on the woman's use of diaphragm, cap or sponge.

Using condoms can be a hassle. You can sacrifice some sensitivity, you may both feel, as well as run the risk of killing the moment. Better kill the moment than you! A few moments of discipline initiated safely before this most heated and passionate of times potentially might save *both* your lives.

Although its reality remains a nightmare, and patients suffer terribly and deserve our unconditional support, the advent of AIDS has probably provoked an unwarranted emphasis on sexual disease. The cop-out clarion call by governments, media, medics, *et al* for "safe sex" (i.e. using a condom) merely feeds demand for casual and irresponsible sex, driving a wedge through the social fabric that was once society's main protection from disease and unwanted progeny.

What do these pundits say to do when you both want to start a family? Think carefully. Hopefully you will do so in time to recognise the importance of honesty, integrity and a decent reputation, rather than behave in some wanton manner on the back of such a simplistic edict.

PENILE PROBLEMS

Measuring up

Broadly (sorry) speaking, telling a man not to worry about the size of his penis is like telling a woman not to worry about her weight. Lack of an acceptable means of direct comparison means that the flaccid state of your penis in the communal showers is about the only "proof" that you will ever find that everybody might be better blessed than you are. However, that ignores the surprisingly large differences in erectile expansion which can flatter the "small" man disproportionately.

The common consensus among women, whether they tell

you or not, is that size does matter. However, they quickly add that the ability to maintain an erection, to recover quickly after orgasm, strength in foreplay and the right sexual attitude are really much more important. To women, the size when at rest is largely irrelevant. Unless you really believe you are one of a tiny number of men whom surgery might help, forget all about it.

Wanting a female partner who is a paragon of virtue can amount to sexual hypocrisy. You may need to accept, if she is the same age as you, that she has had similar, if not more, sexual experience than you have. Try to put any worry about matching up against her ex(es) into perspective. Not only may she be wondering if she matches up to your previous partner(s), if any of hers was so fantastic, why isn't she with him any more? By the way, try not to ask her what she thinks of your dimensions. You might not like the answer.

Impotence

Failure to achieve an erection happens to most men at some time. You don't qualify as impotent, however, when the real cause is a skinful of booze. Genuine impotency on the other hand means frequently experiencing the inability to produce or maintain an erection for no readily apparent reason.

Underlying causes may be physical or psychological. You may need a word with your doctor to help decide which and then receive appropriate, proper treatment. Some medications, unfortunately, do affect sexual functions.

On the psychological front, inexperience, tiredness, anxiety, low confidence, depression, stress, or even sexual excess, can all take their toll but not usually for too long. You will spring back after a few hours or days of abstinence.

Hopefully, we have removed some of these pressures, should they apply, from your first-time sex. Try also to place yourself in situations where you can spend time getting comfortable with your partner. Your place, her place or overnight neutral ground, it doesn't matter where, so long as time will not be in short supply. Avoid being rushed in any way.

Premature ejaculation

Quick-draw shooting makes great viewing in spaghetti westerns, but may be a cause for concern in the bedroom. Inexperience can be a cause but it is more usually, we would suggest, triggered by being over eager; however, semen build-up during droughts of sexual inactivity can eventually also have the same effect.

Being over eager may be just that or may perhaps be linked to some apprehension as to her reactions to your sexual prowess or lack thereof. Counselling can greatly ease this sort of hidden agenda.

However, she can help you greatly too, if you tell her the state of play. Whenever you feel your crescendo building close to the point of ejaculation, you both need to disengage from any penile friction while you let those feelings subside. You can allow your erection to subside too, or not, perhaps according mainly to its own will. What matters is that you insert a delay. A few moments may suffice or a longer time be chosen; the main thing is to be in touch with each other's feelings so that this simple time delay, repeated as needed, can ward off ejaculation until you are both wanting it.

FOREPLAY

Extending foreplay with some gaps and plenty changes to the areas of stimulation is undoubtedly the best way to overcome common and temporary penile problems. It should really be titled "play" because you should never lose sight that a woman can be satisfied by this activity alone.

Mouth to mouth

Kissing is vital to good foreplay. There are a variety of ways that women will kiss, so don't just ram your tongue in; wait until she does. While your mouth is working, your hands should also be gainfully employed. Run them up and down her body, squeezing, tracing, and rubbing as you go. When women talk of men as good kissers, they are talking about more than just mouth movement.

If the clothes are on, your touch may need to be quite firm to register but you should never be rough.

Skin to skin

Clothed sex can be quite erotic and it is always best if she is highly aroused before you are undressed. Women are often reluctant to undress in front of men so you should take the lead if she is not forthcoming. Gently pull at her top or unbutton her blouse and make moves to remove your clothing. Comply with any request to turn off lights but unless you're mechanically-minded, let her be the one to remove her bra. Some of the fastenings can make you feel like you have ten thumbs. Panties are a different matter and you can have enormous fun taking these off.

The skin is the largest erogenous zone of all, so please don't target her vagina or clitoris as if it's the only source of stimulation. Run your tongue up and down the small of her back, a neglected area of intimacy. Suck her fingers, lick her neck, the inside of her thighs, kiss her breasts and don't leave your hands static either. Try and keep your touch light, especially in the sensitive breast and labia areas, but her buttocks can normally stand a firm squeeze. No need to leave your penis out of the action either. Rub it against her labia and enjoy the mutually pleasing sensation, but take care not to rip your condom.

Clitoral stimulation is essential for bringing a woman to orgasm by foreplay alone. Modern women do not see masturbation as inadequate or unclean sex, any more than you might consider a female "hand job" to be unfulfilling. If statistics are to be believed, 75% of women have experienced genital stimulation at some time and just as many have enjoyed the pleasure of oral sex. To bring her to orgasm by hand, start with long, slow and gentle rubs, increasing the tempo gradually. Once aroused, she will allow you to rub faster, but, as ever, avoid rushing. You are not rubbing brass.

If you decide on oral sex (and despite all the hype you don't have to), use the same slow/fast finish technique and lap your tongue for all its flexible worth. Both methods take time, so don't abandon the job just because it doesn't look like it's working. Use your free limbs to explore other reachable body parts; then, once she's approaching orgasm, concentrate on the matter in hand or mouth.

CAUTION: HANDLE WITH CARE
Never blow in to the vagina. This can cause potentially fatal air-bubbles, known as embolisms, to develop in the blood-stream.

Stop fumbling about! Rather than us drawing diagrams or giving the location of a woman's most erogenous zone in terms of longitude and latitude, it'll be easier for you to locate in first-time sex if you remember the female genitalia is in the same anatomical position as that of the male. All men and women develop from the same androgynous-looking embryo and it is not until around six weeks after conception that noticeable sex organs start growing. In adulthood the spine of the scrotum is the gender-reverse of the vagina, and the base of the penis (allowing for substantial adjustments in size) mirrors the site of her clitoris. Focus on this general area and you will find it before long.

COITUS
Despite what you may believe, she's not expecting you to try out all the positions of the Karma Sutra. Don't feel inadequate if you're not a bedroom gymnast. The missionary position is standard practice for first-time sex. If she indicates that she wants otherwise, then go with the flow. No matter what the position, the point of entry remains the same. If you want to try something don't be shy, but always respond reassuringly if she signals discomfort. She may not be a bedroom gymnast

either. With good foreplay, it shouldn't be a problem to enter her, but try to resist pumping straightaway. The first thrust is highly arousing for a woman so give her a second or two to enjoy it.

Sexual rhythm is the one area beyond that where we cannot advise, being highly dependent on the desires of both participants. Some women want it hard and fast from the word go, while others prefer a slow, deliberate build up. Thankfully, women are at their most expressive in this area and will often give verbal or physical clues to the tempo they prefer.

AFTERPLAY

Men's annoying habit of falling asleep after sex has been linked (though there is not yet proof) to a hormonal flooding that occurs at orgasm. Women seem to have higher base levels of the hormone involved so its effects are not as great. However, try to fight nature. Give her a post-coital cuddle before she asks for one and accommodate any need she has for conversation. Some women won't want to be held after sex, but they are rare.

When to leave? Don't rush off if you can help it or unless she asks you to. If it's your place, don't push her. Allow her to stay the night and, if it pleases you both, make her breakfast.

When to contact her? We urge no later than the next day if you haven't fixed a definite date. Why play telecommunications games at this point? Sex changes things, no matter what the hardened members of the "fun and run" club say and, if she wants to continue seeing you, she will appreciate such contact.

What if she wakes up next day not wanting an ongoing relationship?

What's wrong with modern women? Isn't one man enough any more? We play devil's advocate here but, according to science, it never was. There is the quasi-logical idea that sperm competition might not exist if women were totally monogamous, and then there is the speculative female gambit of cuckoldry, where a woman expects the emotional and material benefits of a long-term partnership while still having a lover or lovers outside. These lovers may have genetically-appealing qualities, such as looks and competitiveness which a woman may feel are lacking in her partner.

Also coming in to the reckoning, it could be argued, must be the intensive carnal conditioning to which women have been subject in recent years. Perhaps the most widespread is the disingenuous "he would, so you should" argument, beloved by hackademics, glossy magazines and ill-matched peer groups. This guilt-lessening philosophy can be very persuasive, especially when coupled with propaganda about total freedom of relationship choice. Together, these two schools of thought can make any woman feel that one man is never enough, even if she's not a natural bed-hopper. So it seems possible, if not probable, that certain women will take sex and later reject a man, not just because he hasn't got what it takes, but also because they may perceive that the grass is always greener elsewhere.

Sadly, the younger she is, the likelier she is to be part of this "missing out" mindset. Ridding her of such nonsense is beset by the problem that she is unlikely to want to tell you about it. She needs to be free to find out for herself or some part of her will always resent you for having known it all along.

Ultimately, men of reasonable honour have to face up to the fact that some women are simply out playing the numbers game. You sometimes find yourself in the position that her agenda has never included looking at you with long-term eyes, even if the sex was fantastic.

Sometimes you may gamble that a woman you fancy will not turn out this way – usually against your better instinct. If you lose, you will need your strongest will. The only logical move you have is to drop her as soon as you see the light.

What if you don't want a continuing relationship?
Well, it's an imperfect world of which you and we are members. There's no escaping the fact that you can find

yourself less committed to developing a relationship once the initial heat dies down. It's highly unlikely you would be reading this book if you are a man who readily loves and leaves but there's no point in damning yourself with guilt if it has to happen. What's done is done. Now it must become a damage limitation exercise to protect her ego by letting her down as gently as possible. Before you do that though, are you absolutely, stone-cold, sure that you don't want a relationship with her? If your soul-searching reaches the same conclusion as before, then do the decent thing and tell her before any other female can distract you. The easy, lousy option is not to contact her, and is outside the scope of this book.

There is no bombproof way to end a relationship, one such as the above being no exception. The best you can do is accept blame for your part and always do so face-to-face. Tell her that *you* have a problem with commitment, that you *do* like *her* (otherwise you wouldn't be crawling across broken glass now!), that you're sorry for leading *her* on (yes you did) and that, even though you still find her attractive, you won't ever flirt with her again. She may not believe your remorse; the conversation may overheat; she may crank up your guilt by pleading for another chance; but such are the emotional risks of affairs of the heart. The kind of risks the Department of Health won't warn you about. At least you must try to ease her pain, which is more than all too many men will bother.

VIRGINITY

Yours

So you're a virgin? Big deal. Who hasn't been? Understandably you're anxious about your performance when the time (excuse the pun) comes, but you're not alone – although authentic statistics on virginity don't exist to prove this.

What if she guesses? Current research shows that only 13% of women have no knowledge of whether or not their partner was a virgin when they first had sex. However, if you use the techniques described in this chapter, you will probably put her off the scent. The younger she is, the less likely she is to know. Moreover, it has been discovered that 37% of female virgins had first-time sex with a man who was also a virgin. So there is a welcome element of mutual self-discovery at large.

It is also more likely that you will lose your virginity during a permanent relationship than, as many men imagine, on a one night stand. Research shows that 42% of men and 52% of women support this finding. The most common plot, for either sex, is to wait until the right person comes along, to develop a good relationship and a relaxed sexual rapport before going any further.

One further piece of advice – don't expect your penis to find its own way in. Just like fitting an electric plug into its socket, you will have to guide it by hand.

Hers

Please repress all those cynical thoughts. Not all female virgins are found in convents. The majority of women will have experienced orgasm before intercourse (yes, the same way you have) but the actual dynamics of sex with a man are at once an exciting and frightening prospect that needs to be dealt with with tact and diplomacy. That is, of course, assuming you know. Pride may stop her telling you in the same way that it may have stopped you. Reassurance is essential in this situation.

SPECIAL NEEDS

Resistance

It's going against the grain for a man to stop what he's started, but women are much more easily turned off and you *must be prepared to give way*. She may not like a certain aspect of your technique, or she may feel she is being too easy (yes, even at this late stage); you may have broken wind at precisely the wrong moment; she may have deep-held negative feelings about a past relationship which have inexplicably re-surfaced; or she may be an undeclared virgin. It doesn't matter what the reason is, even if your penis has got hard enough to cut diamonds, you must stop. It is highly unlikely that she is just being manipulative, so emphathise and wait. If you are able, openly discuss her reasons for stopping; with patient reassurance, she may allow you to continue a little later. You'll just have to see how this situation develops, leaving sex out of it for the meanwhile.

Kinky sex

The point of using such a provocative heading is to test the openness of your mind. Words like ''kinky'' and ''normal'' are only relative. The only thing that's considered abnormal these days is probably a single women who doesn't mind having sex without a condom.

If you have a penchant for trying sex that is not openly discussed, be advised that experimentation needs, above all, a like-minded partner. Even a simple thing like talking dirty is best left until you know her really well.

9

ENDING AND STARTING

SUCCESSFULLY SINGLE

We have considered everything in stages but, in the whizz-bang world of modern intimacy, you could almost run through this whole book in one encounter. Be flexible. And be careful too. The vital power of attraction contained here is deceptively dangerous, not least because you can become addicted to the ease with which women warm to you. This particularly applies to relationships with partnered women, who warm quickly to confident men, without any of the "Is he the one?" neurosis of single women. There is, unfortunately, a competitive lure involved in being with another man's partner, but please try to resist it. Getting hooked on women with partners will eventually lead to possession problems, friendship break ups and shedloads of guilt. You will also find it difficult to trust any future partner.

This much should be *self*-evident but *self*-discipline is also needed too so you don't get carried away with the bachelor life. If you find the "one", we urge that you do think hard about staying with her, even if some mischievous voice is suggesting that you haven't yet sown all your wild oats.

Backlash from others can be surprisingly volatile. The successful, smiling bachelor seems to be a threat to some people, perhaps jealous of how he seems to be able to take in his stride both forming relationships and passing time without any partner. Your confidence about the former, of course, is part and parcel of your ease about the latter.

Another plus side of being comfortable with women, and more in control of your relationship fate, is that it does help you appreciate how true misery has little or nothing to do with being single. Those who would have you believe otherwise simply diminish their own chances in love and life.

Despite this, some women still seem to see any man who is unabashed about his solo status as a target for levelling! (How dare you be single and self-confident when loneliness, or even just the thought of it, can rip such a huge hole in her well-being?) Problems like these can run deep. Always be aware, should you decide to chase, that they may just be ones you cannot hope to resolve on your own.

All you can usually do about male jealousy is try not to be smug.

Even your best friends may find it hard to adjust to new-found skills and a confidence with which we hope we may have helped. Give them time. But you need not tolerate any spiteful niggling that persists. Cut friends like that loose, whichever sex they are.

MAINTAINING RELATIONSHIPS

It does take a certain amount of gall to write a book like this, but our egos are not so inflated that we believe we know it all. We thought we did, at one time, after initial bursts of relationship success. Then we began to meet women who didn't need us as much as we needed them, and we learned the brutal truth: if the needs don't balance, the relationship is doomed. Striking a balance is difficult but there is much running in your favour, even in these pressurised times of expectation on men.

Adult women take choice very seriously. If she has committed to you past the honeymoon period of forgiving all faults, if you have followed the major principles of giving, respect, friendship and so on, she probably won't want the relationship to end any more than you do. Therefore, even though you may ultimately have to give more than you *feel* you receive in the relationship, you can take comfort from the outset that she will be willing to compromise too.

For the record, two of the authors are currently in long-term relationships, one of them shortly to be married. Though there are peaks and troughs, their partners always know that commitment cannot be all one-way. It is, by its very nature, conditional on mutual concessions. Even the single author (no, not the ugly one), despite his solo status, insists on mutual respect from day one.

Power

Emotional

At the risk of undue (or out of context) quotation, we advise that you should never give a woman as much power as she wants, but never give her less than she feels she deserves either! For example, if you raise your eyebrows when she flirts but she tells you, in private and with a smile on her face, that she thinks you're jealous; just shrug and don't argue. All she's looking for is confirmation that you care. However, if her friendliness with another man were to go beyond propriety, you need to take action. As always, give her the option to change by telling her you don't like it. That should be the end of the affair – no pun intended! However, if she merely carries on unabated, you may have to call time and reject her. How you do this will depend on how long you've been together. The longer that is, and the more flagrant any breach of trust may have been, the more seriously you will want to consider your position and what you are now going to do.

However, not all such issues will warrant rejection. Usually, just holding back on giving attention will prompt an apology from her.

Nonetheless, confrontation is sometimes essential. How is she going to stop overstepping your major boundaries if she doesn't know where those boundaries are?

Don't worry about being seen as a strop or stubborn. What you must keep in the forefront of your mind is that, while there's no shame attached to pleading your utmost for the right woman to stay or crying if she leaves, any man – or woman – who is *totally* unable to put personal dignity before his or her desire for a relationship to continue, is opening the door to abuse. See yourself as nothing outside a relationship and she will eventually see you as nothing inside it. Let her know she is number 1 by showing her that you do more for her than anyone else but, equally, specify that – sometimes – your family (of whom ultimately she may become a part), work (from which she may benefit) and your friends (those who provide meaning and roots to your life) will come first.

Practicalities
She may be better than you at DIY or car maintenance, quite apart from the presupposed differences in cooking skills, housework, or budgeting. Find out who's better at what, because you will soon have to be able to trust each other to complete tasks in your respective areas of talent. You get more done this way and only need to put two heads and hands together for the major decisions or projects. She may be better than you at most things, but no-one is perfect – a small matter, really – but one each of you may need to recognise more than you expect. Rest assured you will have your moments in the sun. You *must* take money seriously. If you really want a relationship to have a premature end, then be lazy about earning, talk about your big plans without doing something to realise them, and let her pay for everything.

Otherwise, our recipe for harmony is (especially if she earns more than you) to turn down every third offer of financial help so that she doesn't feel taken for granted, to accept that she can call some or even *most* of the financial shots and to avoid showing *too* much enthusiasm for being a house-husband – even if it's the only sensible option.

CAUTION: HANDLE WITH CARE
A truly intelligent and capable girl will compromise with a less gifted partner without making him feel inadequate.

However, some such women will still revel occasionally in the ego boost they get from humiliating you. Can you handle her needs in this direction at their current level? She probably won't be willing to stifle them much more and, in the longer run, there might be a downside that they could get worse.

Never take her for granted
Even if she turns out to be the strong one in your relationship, she will sometimes need help too. Learn to spot her personal signs that should warn you she's out of her depth: for example, lip quivers, huffs or long silences. Give her your full appreciation when she goes out of her way to help you over a weak spot.

Be careful not to take *everything* said at face value. When she's ill but says, "It's okay, you can go out with your friends"; when she's taken a day off specially but says, "We don't have to spend the whole time together"; when she's down about her age and says, "Don't bother getting me anything for my birthday"– have the insight to know she may not mean what she says. Women may dislike excessively perceptive men, but they sure like a man who can show compassion and understanding without them having to spell out their feelings.

Never bear grudges
You will argue and you will row, but try to pre-empt ongoing conflict by dealing with a situation then and there (excepting where so doing might humiliate her publicly). More important still, in our experience, don't refer to it again. That's the harder bit.

Women remain the more self-aware sex, so each time you nag her, or bring up a blunder that she thought was forgotten, you only hammer a nail into her self-esteem. Instead you'll need to become fluent in "caretalk", that language of high diplomacy: "I like the way you did that but maybe it would work more simply this way"; which is also capable of letting her down gently – "No, of course you're not putting on weight but, if you want, we could both join a gym". Caretalk takes effort, but if you can manage it, and time it when she's in reflective mood, the chances are that she will learn to use it too.

See her for what she is – rather than what you want her to be

The minor things, different musical tastes or her not caring about the sport you love, can easily be overcome but, never blind yourself to any major incompatibilities. If she wants much more power than you're prepared to give, if she expects you to pay for everything, if you're always a punchbag for her moods, if she's always trying to get you jealous, if she constantly compares you negatively with her ex(s), if you feel that you're the only one compromising, if you've discussed these problems with her and nothing changes, then you may have to accept the relationship isn't going to succeed. All relationships can be hard work some of the time and you should never give up at the first sign of trouble, but if you're always rowing, if you hardly ever feel content, something is *fundamentally* wrong. And then it will be the little things that niggle later on. Even if she is young enough to accept change, are you patient enough to wait for the time it may take? Always remember she may be the mother of your children some day. If things between you are stressful now, what are they going to be like when you have a baby to think about?

Many women can hide tendencies that they know would put men off from the start, both skilfully and over a considerable time. Alcoholism and drug abuse are examples. Other character defects might be criminality or habitual lying.

Should you see signs of such deep-seated problems and she is prepared to discuss them and seek professional help, there may prove to be no need to write her out of your life. However, if she is not willing to go for help and these defects are only going to pull you in as well, it will be time to leave.

Support her ambition

Encourage her realistic ambitions, even if her achieving them may mean she will eventually out-earn you. Money or achievement may change her, but she won't forget the person who helped her get there. In any event, the lottery of life is such that you may land on your feet financially higher up than your dreams too.

Show some vulnerability

If you're the strong one in the relationship, then be careful not to be *too* strong. Outrageous as it sounds, we'd advise you to make some periodic mistakes (these will probably come naturally anyway ...) and show her your trust by telling her at least one true secret of fallibility that no-one else knows.

Much ado about jealousy

Forgive the focus on jealousy, but you don't have to be a marriage counsellor to know what a pernicious emotion it can be and you may need to manage it. Try to give her space: to go out with her friends, perhaps to go on holiday without you; to allow her to take two-hour phone calls from male friends (and yet put your foot down when necessary, like when the same guy calls every day).

If she deliberately plays jealousy games, however, over some extended period, try to work out her motivation when you eventually confront her. It may just be that a boyfriend once did it to her. This doesn't excuse her behaviour. However, if you can let her see that you're not into such immature games, she should relent. We wrote earlier in this chapter of what to do if she will not desist. Whatever your reaction, do not stoop to playing her at her own game. You will only lose – whatever the result.

After an affair

We're not talking here about flings, one-night stands or drunken snogs, although they, equally, are disloyal, dangerous and, so far as a great many people are concerned, immoral.

Perhaps the best that can be said of them is that they show a temporary lack of self-control.

Constant two-timing, on the other hand, requires conscious effort and cannot be so easily explained. Yes, *we* have cheated, *and* had it done to us, so don't think we're being holier than thou. But who better to lead you through the minefield than guys who have seen the map?

Let's first acknowledge having an affair due to unhappiness for the slim excuse it is. The first rule of integrity surely demands that your intimate partner be first to know should your commitment wane terribly. If you want to leave, then how many depressing months are you going to spend hanging around waiting until someone better turns up? Such fudging won't aid you in finding a new partner anyway.

Every man who forms a relationship has to wake up to the fact that he may one day have to walk away without another woman to go to. That's how [real] life is.

If you do have a fling then don't tell her, no matter how much the guilt may gnaw into your bones.

Just don't do it again.

If you do tell her, be aware you will get no brownie points for your honesty here. A more accurate description of what you are doing, we would suggest, is salving your conscience rather than supporting her. If you had her interests solely at heart, you wouldn't have cheated anyway. If your heart is in the right place now, you will certainly realise the difficult position your admission puts her in. Technically, she knows she should leave you. Emotionally, she knows that little can be more saddening than having to start over.

As for those who constantly cheat for the sake of it, you are greedy and selfish and if she leaves you it's no more than you deserve.

Naturally you will hope that any woman with whom you connect will have the same values. If she does cheat, she may tell you to ease her guilt rather than to hurt you. This is selfish but understandable as in the above reverse situation.

Perhaps you would have preferred it if she had kept her mouth shut but you have to bear in mind that she may have strayed for little more than the lustful reasons that sometimes drive men. We are saying that her behaviour may have been inexcusable but it is not necessarily unforgivable.

What you really have to decide is whether the benefits of being with her outweigh the pain of her cheating and what you must realise is that, no matter what she says, you are giving her implicit carte blanche to cheat again. You might manage to counter this by telling her that you will leave if it happens again *and* that you may decide to leave anyway. Do nothing to soothe her fears of the latter; especially refuse to discuss a timescale or tariff of any kind. Leaving her "on notice" may just be the stimulus she needs to behave better in the future. This may or may not help her rebuild a track record to your satisfaction – something about which it will always be for you to decide.

Perhaps the hardest betrayal to deal with is when you discover she has had an affair even though she doesn't tell you. A tricky situation indeed and dealing with it may depend on whether you think it was a fling or is ongoing. If you start getting silent calls at your shared flat, if she suddenly has a new schedule, then there's not much point in pretending to yourself that it won't happen again. Before you even think of confronting her though, get your own house in order. Make sure you have your facts straight (suspecting her of having an affair simply isn't enough) and be prepared for her to try and ease her guilt by shifting the blame onto you if she admits the affair. Take deep breaths and please keep reminding yourself not to get physical. It might be that you have neglected her, but she should have brought that up with you first, rather than seeking an affair, no matter how little control she says she has over the situation.

Whether you decide to stay or to give her another chance – indeed, if she decides to stay – are intensely personal questions you both might like to consider along with the advice given above. There are no easy answers here. Consider this though. If she didn't tell you, might it be that she doesn't want to lose you?

Let her change you – a bit
Always keep some of your identity and independence but allow her the pleasure of knowing her opinion matters. While none of us would go for cosmetic surgery if our partners requested it (no matter how much it might be needed!) or give up meat just because she's vegetarian, we have all changed hairstyles and fashions, and resisted re-telling certain jokes because we knew it would make them happy. What doesn't hurt you and makes her happy can't be all bad . . .

Sex is important, but it's not everything
If you're prepared truly to share your desires, the sex can only get better. Exactly how far you go depends on how taboo you feel your wishes may be in her terms. Sometimes putting out a feeler beforehand can help. ''I know someone who . . .'' Encourage her to tell you what *she* really wants. Even if you can't comply, at least she knows she can air her feelings with you.

You can help matters greatly by tuning into the times when she is most receptive, and also by letting her know when you just don't feel up to it, rather than resenting her for your having to perform. The amount of sex will naturally decrease with time so don't panic. So long as you still enjoy each other's company, you can get past this awkward stage. Play, reassurance, protection, commitment and romance will eventually replace passion anyway. Give her a cuddle before she asks for one; learn how to massage her; don't just buy flowers to apologise – stand up for her in public, be affectionate in public and even when she doesn't feel she looks attractive, give her a full-on kiss for absolutely no reason at all.

Dealing with moods
This is where humour and patience come into their own. The more unstable she is, we suggest, the less credence you should

give her moods. (Of course, if she is genuinely feeling ill that is a different matter to deal with accordingly.) Even if she's in a massive sulk, do not play up to her by following her into every room and pleading with you to tell her what's wrong. By all means ask her what's up and let her know that you're there to talk but, if she still won't tell you, stick the telly on and leave her to fume it off.

All women need an emotional outlet, so let her know (through your actions, *never* your words) that you are at least resigned to assuming punchbag status in the following four situations: 1) She's ill. 2) Serious emotional crisis (bereavement, redundancy threat, best friend marrying her ex-boyfriend, etc.). 3) When you're really, really, really in the wrong. 4) On certain calendar days.

Lastly, you need not be afraid to let her see your moods but do try not to take out your moods on her.

CAUTION: HANDLE WITH CARE
The key to helping someone through a crisis is to devote yourself to that person's discomfort no matter how useless you may feel (she may push you away when you try to hold her) or how unprepared (you may never have come across her problem before). You won't always be able to heal her hurt but try not to let her surrender completely, even if you have to remind her diplomatically that life goes on.

Avoid the obvious mixed-culture problems
It would be nice to believe that classes and cultures can always meet half-way, but observation demonstrates that one of you usually has to be prepared to give more in this area. The keynote is never to demean her culture; neither should she indulge in degrading yours. Both of you may likewise need to subsume parts of your own culture into that of the society in which you find yourselves.

Family and friends will sometimes, both consciously and unconsciously, seem to discourage mixed culture relationships.

If yours is one, this may sorely test your commitment. You must be her refuge. Make sure you *can* and *will* be that before your feelings begin to run deep.

THE RIGHT PERSPECTIVE

What with employment and divorce statistics, lesbian chic, and all the implications of cloning, the future may look bleak for men. Look again. Demographics, new technology and fads simply do not reveal how even sex-as-power women are now realising, partly through the backlash against political correctness, what most women instinctively know. No-one is automatically entitled to have it all their own way and women's self-interests are still best served by compromising with men rather than antagonising them. The only man who has something to fear from the future then, is one who can't compromise. If you've read this far, that man is surely not you.

   Oh, one last thing. Good luck!

THE RIGHT JOKE FOR THE RIGHT OCCASION

Reduce your friends to helpless peals of laughter with this joke dictionary! Consult the quick-reference subject suitability list, or make use of the A-Z sequence of the book; whether you are searching for a joke about artificial insemination, the birds and the bees, or about camels, cars or cats – you should find it here.

APT AND AMUSING QUOTATIONS

Pungent, pithy, humorous, telling, sage or maybe just cunningly contrived; the judicious use of quotation has given pleasure and attracted interest since time began. Here are over 1,500 Apt and Amusing Quotations which Geoffrey Lamb has skilfully and enthusiastically drawn together by topic from A to Z.

MAN ALONE COOK BOOK

Do you know how to make an omelette, fry some fish or roast a chicken? How do you stop rice going soggy? Help is at hand. Starting from your first shopping trip, Don Tibbenham shows how easy it is to make tasty meals for one – simply double up the ingredients for two, or choose one of the special recipes included for entertaining.

RIGHT WAY
PUBLISHING POLICY

HOW WE SELECT TITLES

RIGHT WAY consider carefully every deserving manuscript. Where an author is an authority on his subject but an inexperienced writer, we provide first-class editorial help. The standards we set make sure that every **RIGHT WAY** book is practical, easy to understand, concise, informative and delightful to read. Our specialist artists are skilled at creating simple illustrations which augment the text wherever necessary.

CONSISTENT QUALITY

At every reprint our books are updated where appropriate, giving our authors the opportunity to include new information.

FAST DELIVERY

We sell **RIGHT WAY** books to the best bookshops throughout the world. It may be that your bookseller has run out of stock of a particular title. If so, he can order more from us at any time – we have a fine reputation for ''same day'' despatch, and we supply any order, however small (even a single copy), to any bookseller who has an account with us. We prefer you to buy from your bookseller, as this reminds him of the strong underlying public demand for **RIGHT WAY** books. However, you can order direct from us by post, by phone with a credit card, or through our website.

FREE

If you would like an up-to-date list of all **RIGHT WAY** titles currently available, please send a stamped self-addressed envelope to:

ELLIOT RIGHT WAY BOOKS, BRIGHTON ROAD, LOWER KINGSWOOD, TADWORTH, SURREY, KT20 6TD, U.K. or visit our web site at www.right-way.co.uk